The Future of Money

The Changing Face of Global Currency

Written by:

Alan E Shields

INDEX

Preface

In this rapidly evolving world, where technology and economics intertwine in increasingly complex ways, the concept of currency – the very bedrock of our economic transactions – is undergoing a monumental transformation. "The Future of Money - The Changing Face of Global Currency" delves into this transformation, exploring the seismic shift from traditional, government-backed currencies to the innovative realm of decentralized digital currencies.

The Genesis of the Idea

This book is born out of a necessity to understand and demystify the world of digital currencies, a realm that is often shrouded in technical jargon and complex economic theories. As we stand at the cusp of a financial revolution, it becomes imperative to disseminate knowledge that is not only comprehensive but also accessible to everyone, regardless of their financial or technical background.

Navigating Through the Financial Evolution

Our journey begins with an exploration of the current financial landscape, marked by its reliance on centralized currencies controlled by governments and central banks. These traditional forms of money, while familiar, carry with them inherent limitations and susceptibilities – from inflation to political manipulation. As we unravel these issues, the narrative naturally shifts towards the emerging alternative – decentralized digital currencies.

The Blockchain Revolution

At the heart of this revolution is blockchain technology, a groundbreaking innovation that promises transparency, security, and efficiency. This book aims to demystify blockchain and its applications in creating currencies that are not just tools for trade, but also instruments of societal change.

Universal Basic Income and Jobs (UBIJ) in the Digital Era

One of the most pivotal discussions in this book revolves around the integration of Universal Basic Income and Jobs (UBIJ) with digital currencies. This concept reimagines social welfare and employment in the context of a digital economy, offering a radical yet practical solution to contemporary economic challenges such as automation and job displacement.

The GlobeTrotter Ecosystem: A Model for the Future

The culmination of this exploration is the presentation of the GlobeTrotter Ecosystem, a meticulously designed model for an ideal digital currency. This system not only addresses the shortcomings of both centralized and current decentralized currencies but also introduces innovative concepts like a self-financing UBI, a hybrid blockchain, and a smart wallet system.

Empowering the People

Through the GlobeTrotter Ecosystem, this book envisions a future where financial power and control are returned to the people, where economic systems are built on the principles of fairness, transparency, and inclusivity.

Objective and Hope

The overarching objective of this book is not just to inform but also to empower its readers. In a world where financial literacy is increasingly crucial, this book seeks to provide the tools and knowledge for individuals to make well-informed decisions about their financial future. It is a call to imagine, understand, and participate in shaping the future of money – a future that belongs to all of us.

A Journey of Discovery

As you embark on this journey through the pages of "The Future of Money - The Changing Face of Global Currency," I invite you to keep an open mind. This is a journey of discovery – of new ideas, innovative solutions, and a glimpse into a future that promises to redefine the very concept of money and wealth in our society.

Chapter 1
The World of Digital Currencies

Historical Evolution of Money

Welcome to the fascinating journey through the evolution of money, a tale as old as civilization itself. In this section, we'll embark on a chronological voyage, tracing the footsteps of humanity's financial past to understand the present and glimpse into the future. From the barter systems of ancient times to the sophisticated digital currencies of today, this chapter lays the foundation for comprehending the transformative leap towards a digital financial era. As we explore the historical milestones, let's unravel how each shift in the monetary paradigm has mirrored the changing needs, technologies, and philosophies of human societies. Prepare to uncover the roots of our financial systems and how they've paved the way for the revolutionary concept of digital currencies.

- **The Dawn of Trade - Barter Systems**: Delving deeper into the era where currency was non-existent, the barter system stood as the backbone of commerce. Imagine ancient marketplaces buzzing with activity, where goods like grains, livestock, tools, and handicrafts were the currency of the day. For instance, a craftsman might exchange a handmade basket for several fish caught by a local fisherman. This direct trade was inherently personal and community-centric. The value of goods was often subjective, influenced by factors like scarcity, demand, and the skill required to produce them. However, the system was not without its drawbacks. The barter system's limitations became apparent when dealing with larger transactions or more complex societal needs. There was no standard measure of value or unit of account, making larger or more abstract transactions challenging.

- **The Introduction of Coins - The Birth of Money**: The creation of coins by the Lydians was a pivotal moment in economic history. These first coins were stamped with official marks to signify their authenticity and value, a revolutionary concept that abstracted the idea of value from the physical goods themselves. This innovation drastically simplified trade, as coins had a consistent value and were widely accepted. This not only made everyday transactions easier but also paved the way for larger-scale economic activities, such as saving, investing, and taxing. Coins also symbolized a shift in power and control, as the entities that minted and regulated coinage – often the ruling authorities – began to wield significant influence over the economy.

- **Paper Money - A Leap of Faith**: The transition to paper money represented a significant shift in the perception of value. In China, merchants and the government initially issued these notes as a promise to pay the bearer in coinage. This transformation required a considerable degree of trust in the issuing authority and the stability of the system. Paper money represented not just a physical object of value but an abstract promise of value, a concept that would become the cornerstone of modern financial systems. Its adoption marked the beginning of a new era, where wealth could be transferred across large distances more easily, facilitating trade on an unprecedented scale. Over time, the concept of paper money spread along trade routes, gradually being adopted by other cultures and evolving into the various forms of currency we use today.

- **Credit Cards - Buying on Promise**: The advent of credit cards marked a significant shift in the concept of purchasing power. Initially, these cards were exclusive and often limited to specific stores or local areas. The idea was simple yet groundbreaking - customers could make a purchase without immediate cash payment, relying on the issuer's promise to pay the retailer. This 'buy now, pay later' approach was not just about convenience; it was a leap in trust and creditworthiness.

The system hinged on the understanding that the consumer would settle their debt at a later date, usually with interest. By the late 20th century, credit cards had evolved into sophisticated financial tools, complete with reward programs, varying interest rates, and global acceptance. This era saw a dramatic change in consumer habits and economic dynamics, as spending became more about future earnings than present assets.

- **The Digital Revolution - Birth of Digital Currencies**: The digital revolution brought about a paradigm shift in the concept of money. The introduction of digital currencies was underpinned by the rapidly evolving digital landscape, which included advancements in computing power, cryptography, and internet connectivity. Digital currencies proposed an innovative approach to transactions - they were borderless, relatively fast, and removed the need for traditional financial intermediaries. The pioneering digital currency, Bitcoin, introduced in 2009, leveraged blockchain technology to ensure security and transparency. This technology enabled a decentralized ledger, allowing for peer-to-peer transactions without the need for a central authority. The implications were vast: reduced transaction fees, increased privacy, and accessibility to financial services for those outside the traditional banking system. The digital currency era not only challenged existing financial institutions but also raised questions about the very nature of money in an increasingly interconnected and digital world.

- **Why Digital Currencies?**: The inception of digital currencies was a response to a growing distrust in traditional financial systems, especially following the global financial crisis of 2008. This crisis exposed the vulnerabilities and inefficiencies of the existing financial infrastructure, highlighting the need for a more resilient and equitable system. Digital currencies offered an alternative: a decentralized approach where power and control were distributed among its users rather than concentrated in the hands of a few large institutions. The appeal of digital currencies lay in their potential to democratize financial transactions, providing more autonomy to individuals and reducing reliance on potentially unstable or untrustworthy intermediaries. The launch of Bitcoin in 2009 was a watershed moment, introducing the world to a currency that was not only digital but also not controlled by any government or central authority. This concept resonated with many who were disillusioned by the traditional banking sector, setting the stage for a new era in the world of finance.

- **The Blockchain Innovation**: Blockchain technology is the revolutionary foundation upon which digital currencies like Bitcoin are built. It's akin to a distributed ledger or a global database that's not stored in any single location, making it both transparent and incredibly difficult to tamper with. Every transaction on this network is verified by a consensus among its participants and then irreversibly logged in 'blocks' of data. These blocks are linked together in a 'chain', forming a complete and unchangeable history of all transactions ever made on the network. This structure addresses two major concerns with traditional banking systems: transparency and security. Unlike conventional banks where transactions can be opaque and susceptible to manipulation, blockchain provides an open and secure environment. Every participant or node in the network has access to the entire transaction history, ensuring unparalleled transparency. Furthermore, the decentralized nature of blockchain means it is not under the control of any single entity, which significantly reduces the risk of fraud and corruption. This innovation not only redefined the concept of currency but also opened up a myriad of possibilities for its application in various sectors beyond finance.

As we conclude this section, it's clear that the journey of money is one of continuous innovation and adaptation. From trading shells and metals to the inception of paper money and now to the digital age, each phase in the evolution of money has been a response to the changing demands of commerce, technology, and society. This historical perspective provides us with valuable insights into how and why digital currencies have emerged as the next step in this evolution. As we turn the page, let's carry forward the understanding that the story of money is not just a record of economic transactions, but a reflection of human ingenuity and societal progress. With this context, we're better equipped to delve into the complexities and promises of the digital currency landscape that awaits us in the next chapters.

The Emergence of Cryptocurrency

In this chapter, we dive into the dynamic and intriguing world of cryptocurrencies, a realm where finance meets cutting-edge technology. As we step into the era of digital currencies, it's imperative to understand the emergence of cryptocurrency, a concept that has revolutionized the traditional financial systems. We'll explore the genesis of this digital phenomenon, starting with the birth of Bitcoin, the first decentralized currency, and unravel how it paved the way for a multitude of cryptocurrencies. This chapter aims to demystify the underlying principles of blockchain technology, the backbone of cryptocurrencies, and examine the factors that propelled these digital assets into the global spotlight. Join us on this exploration of the digital currency revolution, where we'll decode the complexities and highlight the transformative potential of cryptocurrencies.

- **The Genesis of Bitcoin**: The financial crisis of 2008 shook the world, eroding trust in traditional financial systems and exposing their inherent weaknesses. It was in this tumultuous environment that Bitcoin emerged, a brainchild of the enigmatic Satoshi Nakamoto, who in 2008 published the groundbreaking white paper "Bitcoin: A Peer-to-Peer Electronic Cash System." This paper didn't just introduce a new currency; it proposed a revolutionary financial system that operated without any central authority. Bitcoin was designed to be a decentralized digital currency, enabling direct peer-to-peer transactions without the need for intermediaries like banks. This was a bold response to the failures and shortcomings of the existing financial system, offering a vision of a more transparent and equitable financial future.

- **Ideological Foundations of Bitcoin**: The philosophy underpinning Bitcoin was deeply anti-establishment, challenging the traditional role of central banks and governments in controlling currency. This digital currency was conceptualized as a solution to several problems plaguing conventional money – inflation, central control, and susceptibility to financial crises. Bitcoin's design aimed to achieve decentralization in two key ways: firstly, through its operation on a peer-to-peer network, which removed the need for central intermediaries; and secondly, through its limited supply, which aimed to prevent inflation. The underlying principle was to create a financial system based on consensus and cryptographic security, shifting the paradigm of trust from centralized institutions to a decentralized, transparent network.

- **Understanding Blockchain, the Heart of Bitcoin**: Blockchain is the technological marvel that makes Bitcoin possible. It functions as a decentralized ledger, distributed across a global network of computers, each holding a copy of the entire transaction history. Every transaction is verified by the network participants (miners) and added to a new 'block', which is then linked to the existing 'chain' of blocks. This design ensures that once a transaction is recorded, it cannot be altered retroactively, thereby safeguarding the integrity of the entire transaction history. This immutability is one of blockchain's most significant attributes, providing a level of security and transparency that traditional financial systems struggle to match. The decentralized nature of blockchain means that no single entity has control over the entire network, fundamentally altering the way trust and authority are established in financial transactions. This technology not only powers Bitcoin but has also inspired a host of other applications across various industries, redefining the concept of secure, decentralized transactions.

- **The Allure of Decentralization**: The appeal of a decentralized currency like Bitcoin lies in its foundation of empowering users. In the shadow of the 2008 financial crisis, the global populace was disillusioned with traditional banking systems and governmental financial oversight. The centralized nature of these systems had led to a catastrophic economic downturn, eroding public trust. Decentralized currencies presented an alternative model, one where control was distributed among its users rather than a centralized entity. This system promised enhanced transparency, security, and a democratic form of financial governance, aligning well with the growing public sentiment for financial autonomy and resistance against centralized control.

- **Mining – The Democratic Pillar of Bitcoin**: Mining is the critical process that sustains the Bitcoin network. It's not just about creating new bitcoins; it's about maintaining the integrity and security of the entire system. Miners, using powerful computers, solve complex cryptographic puzzles that validate and record transactions on the blockchain. This process is competitive; the first miner to solve the puzzle gets rewarded with new bitcoins, a process that also introduces new currency into the system in a controlled, predictable manner. This decentralization of currency creation and transaction verification was a stark contrast to the centralized control of traditional currencies. It epitomized a shift towards a more inclusive financial system, where anyone with the necessary resources could participate in the maintenance and growth of the currency. This egalitarian approach to financial governance was a significant draw for early adopters and continues to be a defining feature of Bitcoin and other cryptocurrencies.

- **Bitcoin's Early Days and Growth**: In its infancy, Bitcoin was more of a concept than a widely used currency. Initially perceived as a tool for internet enthusiasts and privacy advocates, it found its first practical application in niche online markets, often operating in the shadows of the internet. However, as awareness of its unique attributes grew – its decentralized nature, finite supply, and potential for anonymity – it began to attract a broader audience. The pivotal moment came when its value started to rise, drawing attention from both individual investors and the tech community. Bitcoin's growth was not without challenges; it faced skepticism, regulatory hurdles, and volatile price swings. Despite this, it laid the groundwork for a new financial paradigm, leading to the emergence of various other cryptocurrencies, each aiming to address different needs and markets. This evolution showcased the potential for a new kind of digital asset, transforming Bitcoin from an obscure digital phenomenon to a significant player in the global financial landscape.

- **Legacy of the 2008 Financial Crisis**: The 2008 financial crisis was a watershed moment that changed the global financial landscape. It exposed the vulnerabilities and systemic risks within the traditional banking and financial systems, leading to widespread economic hardship. This eroded public trust in these institutions and sparked a debate about the need for reform. In this context, Bitcoin emerged as more than just a new form of currency; it was a symbol of financial rebellion. It represented a push towards a system where transparency, user autonomy, and decentralization were paramount. The crisis highlighted the dangers of over-leveraged financial practices and opaque decision-making, paving the way for Bitcoin's alternative approach. This new paradigm proposed by Bitcoin was not just a technical innovation but also a socio-economic response to the failings of the traditional financial systems. It offered a vision of a world where monetary transactions were transparent, direct, and democratized, resonating with a global audience disillusioned by the existing financial order.

As we close this chapter on the emergence of cryptocurrency, we're left with a profound appreciation for the groundbreaking innovation that these digital assets represent. From Bitcoin's initial spark to the flourishing ecosystem of diverse cryptocurrencies, we have witnessed a paradigm shift in the way value is exchanged and stored. This exploration has not only highlighted the technological prowess of blockchain but also illuminated the broader implications for privacy, security, and decentralization in the financial world. As we move forward, let's carry with us the knowledge that cryptocurrencies are more than just digital money; they are a testament to the relentless pursuit of financial freedom and efficiency in an increasingly digital age. With this foundational understanding, we are now poised to delve deeper into the nuanced world of digital currencies and their role in shaping our financial future.

Decentralized Currencies - Beyond Bitcoin

In this section, we expand our horizon beyond Bitcoin to explore the vast and varied landscape of decentralized currencies. The world of digital currencies is not limited to just one pioneer; it's a burgeoning universe of innovative, diverse cryptocurrencies each with unique features and potential. Here, we delve into the evolution of altcoins, exploring how they differ from Bitcoin in technology, utility, and vision. This journey into the world of decentralized currencies beyond Bitcoin will uncover the multitude of possibilities that these digital assets present, from smart contracts to privacy-focused coins, and how they are contributing to the reshaping of our digital financial ecosystem.

- **The Rise of Altcoins**: Bitcoin's emergence opened the floodgates for a myriad of alternative cryptocurrencies, each vying to address perceived limitations of Bitcoin or to introduce new functionalities. Ethereum, for instance, emerged as a game-changer with its smart contract capability, enabling automated, decentralized applications. Meanwhile, Litecoin proposed a lighter, faster alternative to Bitcoin, optimizing transaction speed and efficiency. Ripple (XRP) took a different route, focusing on inter-bank transactions and aiming to streamline cross-border payments. These altcoins weren't just iterations of Bitcoin; they represented new visions for the blockchain technology, each contributing to a broader understanding and application of digital currencies.

- **Diversity and Specialization in Altcoins**: The altcoin universe is marked by its rich diversity, each offering tailored solutions to specific challenges. While Litecoin focused on speed and efficiency, Monero and Zcash ventured into enhanced privacy, offering users the option of completely anonymous transactions – a feature that appealed to those prioritizing confidentiality. Others, like Cardano and Polkadot, explored scalability and interoperability, addressing some of the challenges faced by earlier cryptocurrencies. This diversification meant that the cryptocurrency market evolved into a vibrant ecosystem, offering users a multitude of options based on their individual preferences for speed, privacy, cost, and utility.

- **Impact on Financial and Technological Innovation**: The proliferation of altcoins catalyzed significant advancements in both financial and technological realms. On the technological front, the competition among various cryptocurrencies led to continual improvements in blockchain infrastructure, ranging from enhanced security protocols to more efficient consensus mechanisms like proof-of-stake. Financially, the emergence of diverse cryptocurrencies heralded new forms of investment and fundraising, exemplified by the ICO (Initial Coin Offering) boom, where startups raised capital by issuing new tokens. This wave of innovation went beyond mere currency transactions, paving the way for novel applications in fields like supply chain management, healthcare, and digital identity verification, showcasing the transformative potential of blockchain technology across various sectors.

- **Decentralized Finance (DeFi) - A New Frontier**: Decentralized Finance, commonly referred to as DeFi, marks a seismic shift in the financial sector. Built on Ethereum and other blockchain platforms, DeFi extends the basic premise of cryptocurrencies to a whole financial system. This innovative ecosystem encompasses a variety of financial services, from lending and borrowing to insurance and asset management, all operated on decentralized networks. DeFi applications leverage smart contracts to automate and enforce financial agreements, offering a level of efficiency and security that challenges traditional financial systems. Furthermore, DeFi platforms have introduced novel concepts like yield farming and liquidity mining, which have attracted significant attention for their innovative approach to finance.

- **DeFi's Challenge to Conventional Banking**: DeFi's emergence signals a profound transformation in the financial world. It's not just an alternative but a direct challenge to the existing centralized banking system. By facilitating open access to financial services, DeFi allows anyone with an internet connection to participate in a range of financial activities, from earning interest on savings to obtaining loans without the need for a traditional credit check. This inclusivity breaks down barriers that have long existed in finance, particularly for those in underbanked regions. Moreover, DeFi's transparency, facilitated by blockchain technology, ensures that all transactions are visible and auditable by anyone, a stark contrast to the opacity often associated with traditional financial institutions. As a result, DeFi is rapidly emerging as a robust parallel financial system that offers a more equitable and accessible model for global finance.

- **Real-World Examples and Use Cases**: The practical applications of DeFi in the real world are diverse and impactful. For instance, platforms like Uniswap and SushiSwap have revolutionized how users exchange cryptocurrencies, enabling direct peer-to-peer trading without the need for a centralized exchange. This not only reduces fees but also opens up a wider array of trading pairs. Another significant application is in the realm of lending and borrowing. Platforms like Aave and Compound allow users to lend out their cryptocurrencies or take out loans against their crypto holdings, often with much more attractive interest rates than traditional banks. Moreover, these DeFi platforms provide liquidity pools, where users can contribute their assets to a collective fund used for lending or facilitating exchanges, earning passive income through interest or transaction fees. These examples illustrate how DeFi is reimagining traditional financial services in a decentralized and user-empowered framework.

- **Future Implications of DeFi**: The trajectory of DeFi hints at a transformative future for the financial sector. Its potential to democratize access to financial services could level the playing field, allowing people from all economic backgrounds to participate in financial activities that were once exclusive to a privileged few. However, this burgeoning field also faces significant challenges. Regulatory bodies worldwide are still grappling with how to approach DeFi, leading to a climate of uncertainty for both users and developers. Security remains a critical concern, with the decentralized nature of these platforms making them both resilient yet potentially vulnerable to sophisticated cyber-attacks. Furthermore, building trust with a broader audience beyond the current crypto-savvy user base is crucial for mainstream adoption. As DeFi continues to evolve, it will likely spur innovation in financial services, challenge traditional banking models, and potentially reshape the global economic landscape.

As we conclude this exploration of decentralized currencies beyond Bitcoin, we are left with a clearer understanding of the expansive and innovative nature of the cryptocurrency world. This journey has shown us that the realm of digital currencies is rich with variety, each offering unique solutions and advancements. From Ethereum's smart contract capabilities to the privacy assurances of coins like Monero, we've seen how these currencies are not just alternatives to Bitcoin but are entities with their own distinct contributions to the digital finance landscape. As we step forward, we carry with us the knowledge that the world of digital currencies is a constantly evolving space, brimming with potential and ripe for further exploration and innovation.

Introduction to Central Bank Digital Currencies (CBDCs)

In this segment, we turn our focus to a pivotal development in the digital currency space: Central Bank Digital Currencies (CBDCs). As nations across the globe grapple with the advent of cryptocurrencies, many central banks are exploring or actively developing their own digital currencies. This chapter is dedicated to demystifying CBDCs, understanding their potential impact on the global financial system, and distinguishing how they differ from decentralized cryptocurrencies. We'll delve into the reasons behind the rise of CBDCs, their potential benefits, challenges, and the implications they hold for privacy, autonomy, and the future shape of global finance.

- **Defining CBDCs**: Central Bank Digital Currencies (CBDCs) represent a significant shift in the digitalization of money. As digital versions of a country's fiat currency, they are issued and regulated by the central bank, ensuring their legitimacy and legal tender status. This centralization distinguishes CBDCs from cryptocurrencies, which are typically decentralized and not tied to any governmental authority. CBDCs aim to bring the benefits of digital currencies, like ease of transactions and accessibility, while maintaining the stability and regulatory oversight associated with traditional fiat currencies. They could potentially operate on a 24/7 basis, offering real-time financial transactions, and providing an official alternative to the growing popularity of decentralized digital currencies.

- **Technical Aspects of CBDCs**: The technological framework behind CBDCs varies from one country to another, reflecting their unique economic and regulatory environments. While some nations may adopt blockchain technology for its decentralization, immutability, and transparency, others might prefer centralized digital ledger technologies that offer greater control and scalability. The use of distributed ledger technology (DLT) in some CBDCs mirrors aspects of cryptocurrencies, potentially offering improved security against fraud and counterfeiting. However, the degree of centralization in these systems can greatly impact user privacy and the level of surveillance a government can exercise over financial transactions.

- **Motivations Behind the Creation of CBDCs**: The surge of interest in CBDCs by governments worldwide is driven by a blend of factors. One primary motivation is the need to adapt to a rapidly digitizing global economy, where digital payments are becoming the norm. CBDCs offer a way to streamline payment systems, making them faster, cheaper, and more efficient. Additionally, they present a strategic response to the growing influence of decentralized cryptocurrencies, which some governments view as a threat to their monetary sovereignty. By introducing CBDCs, governments aim to retain control over the monetary system, ensuring stability and mitigating risks associated with digital financial assets. Furthermore, CBDCs have the potential to enhance financial inclusion, especially in regions where access to traditional banking is limited. By providing a digital currency that doesn't necessarily require a bank account, CBDCs could help bring financial services to the unbanked or underbanked populations.

- **CBDCs and Global Finance**: The integration of CBDCs into global finance could be transformative. By enabling faster and more efficient cross-border transactions, CBDCs could significantly reduce the time and costs associated with international money transfers, which traditionally pass through multiple intermediaries. This efficiency could bolster international trade and global economic integration.

However, this shift also presents challenges. For example, CBDCs could disrupt the current balance in foreign exchange markets, potentially affecting exchange rates and international financial stability. Furthermore, the widespread adoption of CBDCs may challenge the dominance of traditional currencies like the US dollar in international trade and finance, leading to a reconfiguration of global financial power dynamics. There's also the possibility of creating new forms of financial exclusion or dependencies, as countries with less developed digital infrastructures might struggle to keep pace with this new financial paradigm.

- **Impact on National Sovereignty**: The deployment of CBDCs is a double-edged sword in terms of national sovereignty. On one hand, they offer nations unprecedented control over their monetary systems. This control could enhance a government's ability to implement effective monetary policies, combat financial crimes, and ensure financial stability. CBDCs could also provide a more precise tool for managing economic crises, such as directing stimulus funds directly to citizens' digital wallets. On the other hand, this increased control comes with significant concerns about privacy and individual freedoms. The digital nature of CBDCs means that transactions could be easily traceable, potentially leading to increased surveillance and governmental oversight of citizens' financial activities. This raises critical questions about the balance between national security, economic stability, and individual rights, particularly in nations with weaker democratic institutions or those prone to authoritarian tendencies. It also highlights the need for robust legal frameworks and safeguards to protect citizens' privacy and prevent misuse of financial data.

- **Examples of CBDC Development**: Around the world, the exploration and adoption of CBDCs are unfolding in varied ways. China's digital yuan, known as the e-CNY, is one of the most advanced examples. The pilot programs in major cities and during major events, like the Winter

Olympics, showcase its potential for widespread retail use. In contrast, the European Central Bank's consideration of a digital euro is in a more exploratory phase, focusing on assessing the benefits and risks before proceeding to development. The Bahamas' Sand Dollar is another notable example, already fully deployed as a means to improve financial inclusion in its archipelago. These diverse approaches reflect differing national priorities and economic contexts. Some countries focus on enhancing domestic retail transactions, while others aim at improving cross-border payments or addressing specific challenges, such as financial inclusion in less densely populated or remote areas.

- **Future Outlook for CBDCs**: The future trajectory of CBDCs is poised to be a significant factor shaping the global financial landscape. As more countries progress from research to pilot programs and full deployment, we can expect CBDCs to influence everything from daily retail transactions to international trade and monetary policy. Key areas of impact include increased financial inclusion, as digital currencies can reach populations underserved by traditional banking. However, challenges such as interoperability between different CBDC systems, maintaining financial stability, and addressing cybersecurity risks will be crucial for their successful integration into the global economy. Additionally, the potential of CBDCs to reshape central banks' roles and functions could lead to a new era in monetary policy, where digital currencies offer novel tools for economic management. The evolution of CBDCs will likely be shaped by ongoing dialogues between regulators, technologists, economists, and the public, ensuring that they not only harness technological innovation but also align with broader societal goals and values.

As we conclude our exploration of Central Bank Digital Currencies, we have gained a more nuanced understanding of this emerging phenomenon in the world of finance. CBDCs represent a significant step by central banks to blend traditional financial systems with the innovations of digital currency technology. However, as we've seen, they also bring forth complex questions about privacy, control, and the changing dynamics of money in the digital age. The future of CBDCs remains a fertile ground for debate and analysis, reflecting the evolving nature of money and its role in society. The journey through this landscape of CBDCs underscores the importance of staying informed and engaged as these new forms of currency continue to take shape and influence our world.

Technology as a Disruptor in Finance

In this part of our exploration, we delve into the dynamic role of technology as a game-changing force in the financial world. This chapter examines how innovations, particularly in digital currency, are radically reshaping the traditional landscape of finance. We'll explore the various ways in which technology is not just a tool but a disruptor, creating new financial models, altering consumer behavior, and challenging regulatory frameworks. Prepare to journey through a world where technology redefines the boundaries of finance, ushering in an era of unprecedented change and opportunities.

- **The Digital Revolution in Finance**: The digital revolution has dramatically transformed the financial sector. The introduction of digital encryption provided the necessary security for online transactions, allowing sensitive financial data to be transmitted safely over the internet. High-speed internet connections facilitated real-time, global financial interactions, breaking down geographical and time barriers. Cloud computing further revolutionized this landscape by providing scalable and flexible resources for handling vast amounts of financial data. These technological advancements have been pivotal in creating a fertile ground for the development of digital currencies, enabling fast, secure, and global financial transactions that were once unimaginable.

- **Blockchain: The Foundation of Digital Currencies**: Blockchain technology, often hailed as the backbone of digital currencies, has redefined concepts of data storage and security. It operates as a decentralized ledger, distributing data across a network of computers, which collectively validate and record transactions. This architecture ensures that each transaction is transparent and immutable, creating a tamper-proof record. Blockchain's ability to maintain a secure and transparent record without the need for a central authority challenges the traditional financial systems, which often rely on central record-keeping entities. It offers an alternative that is not only more secure but also more efficient, as it removes the need for intermediaries in financial transactions.

- **Decentralization: Shifting the Power Dynamics**: Decentralization, a key feature of blockchain technology, fundamentally alters the power dynamics in the financial world. Unlike traditional financial systems, where banks and financial institutions hold centralized control, blockchain distributes power across its network. This shift challenges the long-standing model of financial governance and opens up new possibilities for financial operations. Decentralization reduces the risk of systemic failures and frauds that can occur in centralized systems and democratizes financial participation, allowing individuals greater control over their financial transactions. Moreover, it fosters an environment of innovation, as developers and entrepreneurs can build and deploy financial services and products without the need for traditional financial infrastructure or intermediaries.

- **Immutability: Building Trust in the System**: The concept of immutability in blockchain is a game-changer for trust in financial transactions. Once a transaction is added to a blockchain, it becomes a permanent part of the ledger, immune to alteration or deletion. This level of immutability is a stark contrast to traditional financial systems, where records are often centralized and can be subject to modification or tampering, either through human error or fraudulent activities. In traditional systems, the opaqueness of transaction histories can raise concerns about integrity and reliability. Blockchain's immutable nature assures users that once a transaction is recorded, it remains a verifiable and unchangeable part of the financial history. This characteristic not only enhances security but also builds a foundation of trust among users, crucial in any financial system.

- **Transparency: A New Level of Openness**: Blockchain technology introduces an unprecedented level of transparency in financial transactions. Each transaction on a blockchain is visible to anyone who has access to the network, making it possible to trace the history of a particular asset or currency with ease. This degree of openness is particularly significant in an era where there is growing public demand for transparency and accountability from financial institutions. In traditional banking systems, transactions can be obscured by layers of bureaucracy and privacy policies, making it difficult for consumers to get a clear view of their financial activities. Blockchain's transparent nature allows for a more informed and empowered user base, fostering trust and engagement. This transparency is not only vital for individual consumers but also plays a significant role in corporate governance, allowing for more straightforward auditing processes and reducing the likelihood of corrupt practices.

- **Solving Traditional Financial System Problems**: Blockchain technology addresses several key issues inherent in traditional financial systems. For instance, traditional international remittance processes are often criticized for their high transaction fees and slow processing times, typically requiring multiple intermediaries. Blockchain offers a stark contrast with its ability to facilitate cross-border payments directly between parties, significantly reducing or even eliminating intermediary costs. This not only cuts down on fees but also accelerates transaction speeds. An example of this is the use of blockchain for remittances in migrant worker communities, where funds can be transferred across borders swiftly and with minimal costs, a vast improvement over the traditional banking system. Moreover, blockchain's decentralized nature reduces the reliance on central authorities, mitigating the risk of systemic failures and increasing overall system resilience.

- **The Future of Blockchain in Finance**: Looking into the future, blockchain technology in finance is poised for further revolutionary developments. The integration of artificial intelligence (AI) with blockchain can automate and optimize complex financial processes, such as risk assessment and fraud detection, leading to more efficient and secure financial operations. Moreover, the expansion of blockchain technology is expected to go beyond cryptocurrencies, potentially infiltrating various sectors like supply chain finance, equity trading, and even sovereign debt issuance. These advancements could streamline operations, increase transparency, and reduce costs, further disrupting traditional financial models. In addition, the emergence of more sophisticated blockchain platforms could lead to greater scalability, enhanced privacy features, and improved interoperability between different blockchain systems, paving the way for a more interconnected and efficient global financial infrastructure.

As we conclude our examination of technology's disruptive role in finance, it's clear that the journey has only just begun. The intersection of technology and finance has opened up a realm of possibilities and challenges. From cryptocurrencies to blockchain, these innovations have started to rewrite the rules of financial engagement, democratizing access and empowering users in ways previously unimaginable. As we step into the future, it's essential to keep a keen eye on these technological advancements, understanding that they hold the power to transform not just finance but the very fabric of our economic life and social interactions.

The Impact of Digital Currencies on Traditional Banking

In this insightful segment of our exploration, we turn our focus to the profound impact of digital currencies on the traditional banking sector. As we navigate through this chapter, we will unravel how digital currencies are challenging the conventional banking paradigm, introducing innovative methods of transactions, and reshaping the financial services landscape. This part of our journey invites you to witness the transformative power of digital currencies and their potential to redefine banking as we know it.

- **Disintermediation of Financial Services**: The rise of digital currencies heralds a paradigm shift in financial services, notably in how they could sideline traditional financial intermediaries. Banks, for centuries the stewards of financial transactions, face a fundamental challenge from digital currencies that enable peer-to-peer transactions without the need for a central authority. This change could have profound implications. It questions the long-established banking model and may reduce banks' involvement in daily financial operations. The concept of decentralization in digital currencies, particularly through technologies like blockchain, offers a more democratic financial model where control is distributed among its users, leading to more competitive financial products and services. This disintermediation could also drive down costs for consumers and small businesses, historically burdened by high banking fees.

- **Revolutionizing Transaction Speed and Efficiency**: The speed and efficiency of transactions are among the standout features of digital currencies. Unlike traditional banking systems, where cross-border transactions can take days due to multiple intermediaries and regulatory checks, digital currencies enable near-instantaneous transfers. For example, Bitcoin and other cryptocurrencies can process transactions in minutes, with some newer blockchains achieving this in seconds. This expediency is not just about convenience; it's a critical factor in global trade and finance. Traditional banks, recognizing this shift, are under pressure to innovate and adapt to remain relevant. This could lead to the adoption of blockchain-like technologies in traditional banking or the creation of new financial services that prioritize speed and efficiency.

- **Financial Inclusion: A Path to Empowerment**: Digital currencies offer a groundbreaking solution to a longstanding challenge: financial exclusion. Worldwide, a significant portion of the population remains unbanked or underbanked, primarily due to the lack of access to traditional banking infrastructure, stringent requirements for account opening, and high transaction fees. Digital currencies, with their minimal entry barriers, present an opportunity for these individuals. By using a simple internet connection and a digital wallet, people in remote or impoverished regions can access financial services that were previously out of reach. This accessibility could lead to a surge in economic empowerment and growth in these areas. For example, in regions of Africa and Southeast Asia, where banking infrastructure is limited, digital currencies are already enabling small business transactions, remittances, and savings, showcasing their potential to foster financial inclusion and empower marginalized communities.

- **Cross-Border Payments and Globalization**: Digital currencies are revolutionizing the way cross-border payments are made, aligning seamlessly with the current trends in globalization. Traditional methods of sending money internationally are often slow and costly, involving multiple intermediaries and exchange rate fees. Digital currencies, on the other hand, enable swift and direct transactions across borders at a fraction of the cost. This improvement in efficiency and cost reduction could significantly enhance global trade, fostering closer economic ties and more fluid financial interactions between countries. For businesses, this means faster settlement of international transactions, leading to more efficient global supply chains and operations. Furthermore, digital currencies could democratize access to international markets for small and medium-sized enterprises by lowering the entry barriers. On the flip side, traditional banks are now compelled to innovate, either by integrating digital currency solutions into their services or by developing new financial products that can compete with the speed and cost-effectiveness of digital currencies.

- **The Challenge of Regulatory Compliance**: Navigating the complex regulatory landscape is a significant challenge for digital currencies, especially when juxtaposed with the highly regulated traditional banking sector. While banks adhere to stringent regulatory frameworks that govern everything from customer onboarding to international transactions, digital currencies often operate in a grey area. This decentralized nature challenges existing financial regulations and raises questions about consumer protection, anti-money laundering (AML) efforts, and the prevention of financing illicit activities. However, this also presents an opportunity for regulatory bodies and financial institutions to evolve and adapt. Banks and other traditional financial institutions are exploring ways to integrate the benefits of digital currencies while maintaining regulatory compliance. This could involve developing new compliance models tailored to digital currencies or collaborating with fintech companies to leverage their technological expertise. Furthermore, the rise of digital currencies is prompting governments and regulatory bodies worldwide to rethink and reformulate financial regulations to encompass these new forms of currency, balancing the need for innovation with the necessity of maintaining financial stability and protecting consumers.

- **Reimagining Financial Products and Services**: The emergence of digital currencies is a catalyst for innovation in traditional banking, pushing financial institutions to reimagine their products and services. Banks are increasingly exploring digital wallets, which enable users to store and manage digital currencies alongside traditional funds, offering a blended financial experience. Additionally, blockchain technology is finding its way into loan and payment services, offering more secure and efficient alternatives to conventional methods. For instance, blockchain-based loans can streamline the lending process, reducing paperwork and speeding up approval times, while offering new possibilities for collateral management. Payment services are also being transformed, with banks developing faster and more secure transaction platforms, leveraging blockchain's ability to provide transparent, immutable transaction records. This wave of innovation is not just about competing with digital currencies; it's about harnessing their underlying technologies to enhance and modernize the entire spectrum of financial services.

- **The Future of Banking with Digital Currencies**: Looking into the future, the widespread adoption of digital currencies could lead to a significant transformation in the banking sector. Banks may evolve from traditional storers of value to dynamic facilitators of financial services. In this future landscape, banks could leverage their expertise to become trusted advisors, guiding customers through the complexities of digital currency investments, cybersecurity, and portfolio management. They might also form strategic partnerships with fintech companies, combining their financial acumen with cutting-edge technology to offer innovative services. For instance, we could see the development of integrated platforms where customers manage both fiat and digital currencies, invest in a diverse range of assets, and access a wide array of financial products, all underpinned by blockchain technology. This could lead to more personalized banking experiences, with AI-driven insights and recommendations tailored to individual financial goals and risk profiles. Additionally, the integration of digital currencies into traditional banking systems could lead to more inclusive financial services, reaching unbanked and underbanked populations with more accessible and affordable banking solutions. As banks adapt to this new era, they will play a crucial role in shaping the regulatory and technological landscape of digital currencies, balancing innovation with financial stability and consumer protection.

As we close this chapter on the impact of digital currencies on traditional banking, it's evident that we stand at a pivotal crossroads in financial history. Digital currencies have begun to etch significant changes in the banking sector, compelling traditional institutions to adapt, innovate, or face obsolescence. The ripple effect of these changes extends far beyond banks, influencing economies and societies at large. This chapter leaves us with a clear understanding that the era of digital currencies is not just an emerging trend but a powerful force reshaping the foundational pillars of our financial systems.

Regulatory Landscape and Future Implications

In this essential chapter, we delve into the complex and evolving world of regulations surrounding digital currencies. As these new forms of money gain traction globally, they inevitably encounter a myriad of regulatory frameworks that vary from one jurisdiction to another. This segment is dedicated to unraveling these regulatory landscapes, examining how they impact the adoption and development of digital currencies. Prepare to navigate the intricate interplay between innovation and regulation, a dance that shapes the future of digital finance.

- **The Global Patchwork of Cryptocurrency Regulation**: The regulatory landscape for digital currencies varies dramatically across the globe, reflecting diverse governmental attitudes and economic policies. In Japan, for instance, cryptocurrencies are recognized as legal property, and the country has established clear tax guidelines and regulatory frameworks, promoting a favorable environment for crypto trading and innovation. Contrast this with the United States, where the regulatory environment is more fragmented and cautious, with various federal and state agencies overseeing different aspects of cryptocurrencies, leading to a complex and sometimes uncertain legal environment. On the other end of the spectrum are countries like Bolivia and China, where strict regulations are in place. Bolivia has banned the use of any non-government-issued digital currency, while China, once a hub for crypto activities, has cracked down on all forms of cryptocurrency trading and mining, citing financial risks and energy consumption concerns. This global patchwork creates a challenging environment for international crypto businesses and investors, who must navigate these varying regulations.

- **CBDCs and Government Regulations**: Central Bank Digital Currencies (CBDCs), being government-issued, inherently come with a regulatory framework. This framework offers certain advantages, such as seamless integration with existing financial regulations, including anti-money laundering (AML) measures and know-your-customer (KYC) protocols, which help prevent financial crimes. However, CBDCs also raise significant privacy concerns. Governments could potentially track individual spending and financial activities more easily, which raises questions about state surveillance and individual freedom. The balance between ensuring transaction transparency for regulatory purposes and protecting individual privacy rights is a key challenge in the design and implementation of CBDCs.

- **Balancing Act in Regulation**: Crafting an effective regulatory framework for digital currencies is a delicate balancing act for governments worldwide. Regulators must protect consumers from fraud and ensure the stability of the financial system while avoiding stifling innovation in a rapidly evolving digital currency space. For example, Singapore has emerged as a crypto-friendly hub, with a well-defined but flexible regulatory framework that encourages innovation while ensuring robust consumer protection and financial stability. In contrast, countries like India have taken a more cautious approach, proposing stringent regulations due to concerns over financial stability and investor protection. These case studies highlight the diverse regulatory approaches taken by different countries, reflecting their unique economic contexts, risk appetites, and policy priorities. As digital currencies continue to evolve, the regulatory landscape is likely to remain in flux, with governments striving to adapt to new technologies and market dynamics while safeguarding their financial systems and protecting investors.

- **Innovative Regulatory Approaches**: Around the world, different jurisdictions are experimenting with innovative regulatory approaches to accommodate the rapidly evolving digital currency market. For instance, the UK's Financial Conduct Authority (FCA) has implemented a 'regulatory sandbox' that allows fintech companies to test new financial products and services in a controlled environment without the immediate burden of regulatory compliance. This sandbox approach has been influential, with countries like Australia and Singapore adopting similar models. In regions like Singapore and Switzerland, a "light-touch" regulation strategy has been adopted. These jurisdictions have established clear but flexible regulatory frameworks that encourage innovation in the crypto space while maintaining robust standards for investor protection and financial stability. These innovative approaches reflect an understanding that traditional regulatory models may not always suit the dynamic nature of digital currencies, and a willingness to adapt regulatory strategies to foster technological innovation and economic growth.

- **The Challenge of Cross-Border Regulation**: The global and borderless nature of the digital currency market introduces significant complexities in regulatory efforts. Digital currencies transcend national borders, making it challenging for any single country's regulatory framework to be fully effective. For instance, a digital currency exchange might be based in one country, serve customers in another, and be incorporated in a third, each with its own regulatory standards and enforcement mechanisms. This situation creates a patchwork of regulations that digital currency platforms must navigate, often leading to legal uncertainty and operational challenges. The discrepancies in regulatory approaches can also hinder international transactions, as businesses and consumers must contend with varying rules and compliance requirements across different jurisdictions. This underscores the need for international cooperation and dialogue among regulators, financial institutions, and industry players to develop harmonized regulatory frameworks that address the unique challenges posed by digital currencies while supporting their safe and efficient use globally.

- **Consumer Protection and Security**: The regulatory framework for digital currencies is critically anchored in consumer protection and security. As digital currencies gain popularity, the risks of fraud, market manipulation, and security breaches have become more pronounced. For example, the infamous Mt. Gox hack in 2014, where 850,000 bitcoins were stolen, highlighted the need for stringent security measures and regulatory oversight. Regulatory bodies worldwide, like the Securities and Exchange Commission (SEC) in the U.S., have started implementing regulations to protect consumers against such risks. These include mandating strict Know Your Customer (KYC) and Anti-Money Laundering (AML) compliance for digital currency exchanges, enforcing security protocols, and establishing frameworks for reporting and compensating thefts. In some cases, these regulations have led to the shutdown of exchanges that fail to meet security standards, thereby safeguarding investors' interests. These measures are crucial in building trust in the digital currency market and ensuring its long-term viability.

- **The Future of Digital Currency Regulation**: Looking ahead, the regulation of digital currencies is poised to evolve in several key directions. A significant potential development is international regulatory collaboration, as cross-border digital currency transactions become more commonplace. This may lead to the establishment of global regulatory standards for digital currencies, similar to the Basel Standards for traditional banking. Such collaboration could facilitate more consistent and effective regulation, reducing the risks of regulatory arbitrage where businesses exploit differences between jurisdictions. Furthermore, emerging technologies like AI and blockchain could play a pivotal role in regulation. AI could be utilized for monitoring unusual transaction patterns to prevent fraud and money laundering, while blockchain might offer new ways to track and verify digital currency transactions in real-time, enhancing transparency. The development of central bank digital currencies (CBDCs) could also influence regulatory practices, as governments and central banks might set new standards for digital currency operations. Overall, the future of digital currency regulation is likely to be marked by a combination of technological innovation, international cooperation, and a focus on balancing market growth with consumer protection and financial stability.

Concluding our exploration of the regulatory landscape for digital currencies, it's clear that this is a dynamic and rapidly evolving area. The future implications of these regulations are significant, with the potential to either foster innovation or stifle the growth of this nascent sector. This chapter underscores the need for a balanced approach to regulation, one that ensures security and compliance while also nurturing the growth and potential of digital currencies. As we move forward, the relationship between digital currencies and regulatory frameworks remains a key area to watch, with its outcomes likely to shape the financial landscape for years to come.

As we close this chapter, let's take a moment to reflect on the remarkable journey we've embarked upon. From the ancient barter systems to the innovative realm of digital currencies, the evolution of money mirrors the evolution of society itself. We've traversed through history, witnessing the birth of coins, the adoption of paper money, the convenience of credit cards, and finally, the groundbreaking emergence of cryptocurrencies and Central Bank Digital Currencies (CBDCs).

In our exploration, we uncovered how technological advancements, particularly blockchain, are fundamentally reshaping the financial landscape, challenging traditional banking models, and prompting a reevaluation of the global regulatory framework. The impact of digital currencies extends beyond mere transactions; they are redefining notions of financial sovereignty, privacy, and inclusion.

But as we turn the page to Chapter 2, "The Rise of Blockchain and AI in Finance," let's ponder a thought-provoking question: If digital currencies represent the future of money, how will this transformation affect our daily lives, from the way we purchase our morning coffee to how we save for retirement? Are we ready to adapt to a world where financial transactions are decentralized, faster, and perhaps more transparent than ever before?

The next chapter promises to deepen our understanding of these technologies and their profound implications. We'll delve into the intricate world of blockchain and the burgeoning role of Artificial Intelligence (AI) in finance. As these technologies continue to evolve, they are not just tools for financial transactions but harbingers of a new era of economic operation and interaction.

Join me as we continue to navigate this exciting and uncharted financial landscape, where the possibilities are as limitless as our capacity to innovate. The future of money is not just a concept to be studied but a reality to be shaped and lived.

Chapter 2
The Rise of Blockchain and AI in Finance

Welcome to Chapter 2, where we delve into the transformative impact of Blockchain and Artificial Intelligence (AI) in the financial sector. This chapter explores how these groundbreaking technologies are reshaping the way we think about and interact with money. From decentralized ledgers to intelligent algorithms capable of predictive analytics, we'll discover how blockchain and AI are not just tools of the future, but catalysts of change in the present financial landscape. Prepare to unravel the intricacies of these technologies and their profound implications in finance.

Foundational Concepts of Blockchain Technology

In this section of Chapter 2, we delve into the core principles that underpin blockchain technology, a cornerstone of modern finance. We will explore the fundamental concepts that make blockchain a revolutionary tool, from its decentralized nature to its immutable ledger. This journey will provide a comprehensive understanding of how blockchain operates, laying the groundwork for grasping its profound impact on the financial sector. Prepare to unlock the mysteries of blockchain technology and appreciate its potential to redefine financial transactions.

- **Understanding the Blockchain Structure**: The structure of a blockchain is akin to a digital ledger, but with enhanced security and decentralization features. Each block in the chain contains a cryptographic hash of the previous block, a timestamp, and transaction data, effectively creating a linked sequence. This chain of blocks forms a complete record of all transactions, and once recorded, the data in any given block cannot be altered retroactively without altering all subsequent blocks. This immutability is a key characteristic. The blockchain's decentralized nature means it exists across a network of computers, making it highly resistant to data tampering and providing a robust, transparent, and auditable transaction history. This structure underpins not just cryptocurrencies but a wide array of applications, from supply chain management to voting systems, where secure and transparent record-keeping is paramount.

- **The Role of Nodes in the Network**: Nodes are the backbone of a blockchain network, ensuring its functionality, integrity, and continuity. Every node on the network has the task of validating and relaying transactions and, in many cases, participating in the consensus process. This consensus mechanism, which varies from one blockchain to another (e.g., Proof of Work in Bitcoin, Proof of Stake in Ethereum 2.0), is crucial for maintaining the integrity and agreement across the network on the state of the ledger. Nodes come in different forms: some store a complete copy of the blockchain (full nodes), while others may store only recent parts of the chain or specific information related to the node's functions. The distributed nature of nodes contributes to the resilience of the blockchain against attacks or failures, as there is no single point of failure.

- **Public vs. Private vs. Consortium Blockchains**: The distinction among these types of blockchains lies in their access and control mechanisms. Public blockchains are completely open, where anyone can participate in the consensus process, view transactions, and even develop decentralized applications. They offer the highest level of decentralization and transparency but can face challenges like scalability and energy consumption (as seen in Bitcoin's Proof of Work model). Private blockchains, in contrast, are controlled by a single entity, which makes them more centralized. They are often used within an organization where trust is established, and speed and efficiency are prioritized. Consortium blockchains are a hybrid, governed by a group of organizations rather than a single entity, offering a balance between the trustless environment of public blockchains and the control of private blockchains. This type is particularly appealing in business environments, such as banking or supply chain management, where multiple entities need to collaborate and share data securely and transparently.

- **The Essence of Cryptography in Blockchain**: Cryptography is the bedrock of blockchain's security and integrity. It employs complex mathematical algorithms to encrypt data, ensuring the authenticity and confidentiality of transactions. In blockchain, each transaction is signed with a digital signature, which acts as a personal, unforgeable stamp of identity, created using the sender's private key. This process, known as cryptographic hashing, ensures the integrity of the data within each block. Moreover, the cryptographic link between each block (where each block contains the hash of the previous block) adds another layer of security. This intricate use of cryptography not only safeguards against unauthorized changes but also provides a mechanism for users to verify transactions independently, without needing centralized intermediaries. This cryptographic trust model is what enables blockchain's key features: immutability, transparency, and security.

- **Decentralization: Power to the People**: The decentralized structure of blockchain represents a paradigm shift in data management and distribution. In a decentralized blockchain network, every participant (or node) has an equal level of authority and a complete copy of the ledger, leading to a system where trust is distributed among a vast network of users rather than centralized in a single entity. This democratization of data management significantly reduces risks associated with central points of control and failure. It also empowers users by giving them direct control over their transactions and data. Moreover, decentralization enhances transparency, as all transactions are visible to all network participants, fostering a level of openness and accountability that is often lacking in traditional centralized systems. This decentralized consensus mechanism is not just a technical innovation; it represents a shift towards a more transparent, equitable, and inclusive financial ecosystem.

- **Immutable Transactions for Transparency and Trust**: The immutable nature of blockchain transactions is a cornerstone of its appeal. Once a transaction is added to the blockchain, it becomes a permanent part of the ledger, visible to all participants. This transparency ensures that every transaction can be easily tracked and audited, fostering a high level of trust among users. In finance, where the integrity of transactions is critical, this feature is invaluable. It significantly reduces the likelihood of fraud, errors, and manipulation. For instance, in stock trading, blockchain can provide a clear and unalterable record of all transactions, ensuring fairness and compliance. Similarly, in real estate, blockchain can maintain a transparent history of property ownership, simplifying title searches and reducing fraud.

- **Smart Contracts: The Game Changers**: Smart contracts represent one of the most transformative aspects of blockchain technology. These digital contracts automatically execute, control, or document legally relevant events and actions according to the terms of a contract or an agreement encoded within them. The potential applications are vast and varied. For example, in the insurance industry, smart contracts can automate claim processing, triggering payments automatically when predefined conditions are met, such as flight delays in travel insurance. In supply chain management, they can track the provenance of goods, automatically releasing payments upon delivery confirmation. The automation provided by smart contracts streamlines processes, reduces administrative overhead, and minimizes the potential for disputes. Furthermore, because they operate on blockchain technology, these contracts are secure, transparent, and tamper-proof, adding an extra layer of trust and efficiency to digital transactions and agreements.

As we conclude this exploration of blockchain's foundational concepts, we've equipped ourselves with a deeper understanding of this game-changing technology. It's clear that blockchain is not just a buzzword but a pivotal innovation with the potential to revolutionize how we conduct financial transactions. The knowledge gained here forms the bedrock for appreciating the subsequent advancements and applications of blockchain in finance. As we move forward, these concepts will serve as essential building blocks in our continued exploration of the intersection between finance, blockchain, and AI.

Blockchain's Disruption in Financial Transactions

In this enlightening segment of Chapter 2, we're set to unravel how blockchain technology is redefining the landscape of financial transactions. This chapter takes you on a journey through the myriad ways blockchain disrupts traditional finance, offering insights into its transformative impact on everything from banking to global trade. As we navigate through this section, we'll discover the powerful implications of blockchain's ability to enhance transparency, security, and efficiency in financial dealings.

- **Redefining Trust in Financial Transactions**: The advent of blockchain has introduced a novel concept of trust in the financial sector. In traditional systems, trust hinged on established financial institutions like banks, which acted as central authorities. Blockchain disrupts this model by decentralizing trust; it distributes the verification of transactions across a network, making the system itself trustworthy. This paradigm shift is not just technological but philosophical, altering how individuals and entities perceive and engage in financial transactions. For example, in peer-to-peer lending platforms built on blockchain, borrowers and lenders interact directly, with the technology ensuring the integrity of transactions, reducing the need for traditional credit-checking intermediaries. This change is enabling new forms of financial interactions and collaborations, with a transparency and security that traditional systems struggled to offer.

- **Immutability: A New Standard for Security**: The immutability of blockchain brings a heightened level of security to financial transactions. This feature ensures that once a transaction is added to the blockchain, it cannot be tampered with, creating a permanent and unchangeable record. This aspect is particularly vital in scenarios like international trade finance, where the authenticity of transaction histories is crucial. For instance, blockchain's immutability has been instrumental in tracking the authenticity of goods in supply chains, ensuring that each product's journey from manufacture to sale is accurately and securely recorded. This ability to provide a tamper-proof record is dramatically reducing the instances of fraud and error in financial transactions, from banking to asset management.

- **Transparency: Ensuring Openness and Accountability**: Blockchain's inherent transparency is reshaping the landscape of financial accountability. Every transaction recorded on a blockchain is transparent to all its participants, providing an unprecedented level of openness. This feature is particularly transformative in sectors like corporate finance, where blockchain can offer a clear record of company transactions, investments, and asset transfers, fostering greater investor confidence and regulatory compliance. In the public sector, blockchain's transparency can aid in the monitoring of government spending and aid distribution, allowing citizens and watchdog organizations to track the flow of funds and hold entities accountable. This degree of transparency is helping to build a new financial ecosystem that is not only more efficient and secure but also more accountable and democratic, aligning with modern demands for transparency in financial dealings.

- **Elimination of Intermediaries: Streamlining Processes and Reducing Costs**: The blockchain technology's ability to facilitate direct peer-to-peer transactions has significantly streamlined financial processes. By bypassing traditional intermediaries like banks, brokers, and payment processors, blockchain reduces the layers and associated costs in transactions. This shift is most evident in international trade and remittances, where traditionally high transaction fees and lengthy processing times are greatly diminished. For instance, in remittance transactions, blockchain allows migrants to send money back home more efficiently and cheaply than through conventional banking channels. Similarly, in international trade, smart contracts on blockchain can automatically execute and verify transactions, reducing the need for middlemen, lowering costs, and simplifying logistics. This direct transaction model is not only cost-effective but also increases transparency, reducing the potential for errors and fraud.

- **Increased Efficiency and Speed**: Traditional banking systems, particularly for cross-border transactions, involve complex processes and multiple intermediaries, leading to significant delays. Blockchain technology revolutionizes this by enabling almost instantaneous financial transactions. This efficiency is a game-changer for businesses operating globally, as it allows for faster settlement of trade, improving cash flow and operational efficiency. Consumers also benefit from this speed, especially in contexts like real-time payments, investment settlements, and personal transfers. For example, international payments that would typically take days to process through banks can now be completed in a matter of minutes using blockchain, dramatically accelerating business operations and financial dealings. This enhanced speed and efficiency are pushing traditional financial institutions to adapt and evolve, adopting blockchain technologies to meet these new benchmarks in transactional performance.

- **Smart Contracts in Financial Transactions**: Smart contracts, an integral feature of blockchain technology, are revolutionizing various financial processes. These digital contracts automatically execute and enforce the terms of an agreement, significantly streamlining and automating financial transactions. In the realm of loans, for instance, smart contracts can automatically release funds once the borrower meets certain predefined criteria, reducing the processing time and eliminating the need for manual oversight. In insurance, they enable quick claim processing, automatically verifying and settling claims based on the data input, thus reducing fraud and administrative costs. Similarly, in stock trading, smart contracts can facilitate immediate settlement of trades, bypassing the traditional two-day settlement period (T+2) and thereby reducing counterparty risk. This automation brings efficiency, speed, transparency, and security to financial transactions, making them more reliable and cost-effective.

- **Challenges and Limitations**: Despite the transformative potential of blockchain in financial transactions, several challenges persist. Scalability is a significant concern, as the current infrastructure of many blockchain networks, like Bitcoin and Ethereum, can handle only a limited number of transactions per second, which is far less than what major financial systems process. This limitation poses a challenge for blockchain's widespread adoption in large-scale financial operations. The energy consumption associated with mining activities, particularly for proof-of-work systems, is another critical issue, raising environmental concerns due to the massive electricity usage. Furthermore, the nascent nature of blockchain technology means that regulatory frameworks are still evolving. There is a need for comprehensive regulatory guidelines to manage these new types of transactions, ensure user protection, and prevent illegal activities. As the technology and its applications grow, addressing these challenges through innovation, regulatory adaptation, and infrastructure development will be crucial for blockchain's sustained integration into mainstream financial systems.

As we close this chapter on blockchain's disruption in financial transactions, it's evident that we are witnessing a monumental shift in the finance industry. Blockchain's influence extends far beyond its initial cryptocurrency roots, marking a new era of financial operations characterized by heightened security, improved efficiency, and unparalleled transparency. This exploration has not only illuminated the current state of blockchain in finance but also set the stage for anticipating its future advancements. As we progress, the potential for further innovation and disruption in the finance sector remains an exciting prospect.

Introduction to AI in Finance

In this section of Chapter 2, we delve into the intriguing world of Artificial Intelligence (AI) in finance. AI's integration into financial services marks a revolutionary step towards smarter, more efficient, and personalized financial experiences. This chapter will explore how AI is reshaping the landscape of finance, from automating complex tasks to providing insightful data analysis. As we journey through this segment, we'll gain a deeper understanding of AI's role in transforming financial services and its potential to redefine the future of the industry.

- **AI's Growing Footprint in Finance**: The financial sector is witnessing a significant transformation, with Artificial Intelligence (AI) at the forefront of this change. AI's ability to swiftly and accurately process and analyze vast volumes of data is revolutionizing traditional financial practices. From algorithmic trading to credit scoring and fraud detection, AI's applications are diverse and expanding. By integrating machine learning algorithms, natural language processing, and predictive analytics, financial institutions are enhancing efficiency, accuracy, and decision-making processes. This shift is not just improving existing services but also paving the way for innovative financial products and services. AI's growing footprint in finance marks a pivotal shift towards a more data-driven, automated, and customer-centric financial ecosystem.

- **Machine Learning – The Predictive Powerhouse**: Machine learning, a critical subset of Artificial Intelligence, stands as a technological marvel in the financial sector, employing advanced statistical methods to enable computers to "learn" from and make predictions based on data. In the realm of finance, its utility spans various domains, from predicting stock market fluctuations to assessing credit risks and identifying fraudulent activities. For instance, machine learning algorithms are now adept at scrutinizing vast and complex datasets to forecast stock market trends, often with remarkable accuracy. These algorithms analyze historical and real-time data, learning from market patterns and anomalies to provide investors and financial institutions with actionable insights. Beyond market predictions, machine learning also excels in credit scoring, where it sifts through a myriad of borrower data points to assess creditworthiness, revolutionizing traditional credit evaluation methods. This technology's predictive prowess is not just about efficiency; it's a game-changer in financial risk management and personalized financial services.

- **Natural Language Processing (NLP) in Financial Analysis**: Natural Language Processing (NLP) stands at the forefront of technological advancements in finance, embodying the intersection where computers grasp the nuances of human language. This revolutionary AI technology is adept at parsing and interpreting vast swaths of text from financial reports, news articles, and even the bustling world of social media. In the realm of finance, NLP's prowess is particularly invaluable in dissecting the tone and context of financial discourse to assess market sentiment. By algorithmically analyzing language patterns and keywords within these texts, NLP can uncover underlying investor sentiments and market trends that might not be immediately apparent. For instance, it can sift through earnings call transcripts or CEO interviews to extract subtle cues about a company's future prospects. Similarly, NLP algorithms can scour through social media platforms and financial news outlets, translating the cacophony of opinions and reports into coherent, actionable insights. This ability to decode and quantify subjective information gives investors and analysts a powerful tool to anticipate market movements based on public sentiment, thereby offering a more holistic view of the financial landscape beyond mere numerical data.

- **Neural Networks – Simulating Human Decision Making**: Neural networks, an intriguing facet of Artificial Intelligence, are designed to emulate the intricacies of human cognitive processes, particularly in interpreting complex and multifaceted data patterns. These networks, inspired by the neural pathways of the human brain, are instrumental in decoding the vast, interconnected web of financial information. Their prowess shines in areas requiring rapid and nuanced decision-making, such as high-frequency trading. Here, neural networks analyze a deluge of market data at lightning speed, recognizing subtle patterns and trends that escape human detection. They process this information to make swift trading decisions, navigating the volatile world of financial markets with a precision and speed that outstrips human capabilities. This technology has become a cornerstone in modern financial strategies, allowing traders and investment firms to capitalize on fleeting market opportunities with remarkable efficiency. The application of neural networks in finance is a testament to the growing synergy between human financial expertise and advanced AI, paving the way for more innovative and effective financial decision-making tools.

- **Fraud Detection and Prevention**: In the dynamic realm of finance, Artificial Intelligence, especially through machine learning and neural networks, has emerged as a game-changer in combating fraud. These AI systems possess the remarkable capability to sift through vast quantities of transaction data at unprecedented speeds. By analyzing patterns and trends within this data, they can pinpoint irregularities and deviations that might signal fraudulent activities. This approach is far more advanced and efficient than traditional methods, allowing for real-time detection and rapid response. The precision of AI in identifying these anomalies is pivotal in fortifying the financial sector against sophisticated fraud schemes. This enhanced level of security not only protects financial institutions but also bolsters consumer trust, ensuring a safer and more secure financial landscape. The integration of AI in fraud detection represents a significant leap forward, delivering a robust shield against fraud that was once thought unachievable.

- **Risk Assessment and Management**: In the intricate world of finance, Artificial Intelligence (AI) plays a crucial role in risk assessment and management, a fundamental aspect for any financial institution. AI's advanced algorithms are adept at delving into vast historical data sets and scrutinizing current market trends. This capability enables AI systems to calculate and predict risks with a high degree of accuracy, whether it's for loan approvals, insurance underwriting, or investment portfolio management. For instance, in loan approvals, AI can assess the creditworthiness of applicants by analyzing their financial history and current economic factors, thus providing a comprehensive risk profile. Similarly, in insurance, AI helps in formulating policies by evaluating potential risk factors more effectively. In the realm of investments, AI's predictive analytics play a pivotal role in balancing portfolios by forecasting market fluctuations and identifying high-risk and high-reward opportunities. Consequently, AI empowers financial institutions to make more informed and data-driven decisions, enhancing their ability to manage risk in an increasingly volatile financial environment. This not only optimizes financial operations but also significantly reduces the chances of unexpected losses, thereby safeguarding both the institutions and their clients.

- **Personalized Financial Services**: The advent of AI has revolutionized the way financial services are offered, bringing an unprecedented level of personalization. Robo-advisors, powered by AI algorithms, analyze individual financial situations and goals to provide tailored investment advice, often at a lower cost than traditional financial advisors. AI also powers chatbots and virtual assistants, transforming customer service experiences by providing quick, efficient, and 24/7 support for a range of inquiries, from account balances to complex financial queries. These AI-driven tools are not only more responsive but also continually learn from interactions to offer more personalized and relevant advice over time. Beyond robo-advisors and chatbots, AI enables customization in areas such as credit scoring, where machine learning models assess creditworthiness more accurately by considering a broader range of factors than traditional methods.

- **Algorithmic Trading**: AI has significantly impacted the domain of algorithmic trading, where sophisticated algorithms autonomously execute trades based on set criteria, such as price, volume, or market conditions. These AI systems can process and analyze vast amounts of market data at speeds impossible for human traders, identifying patterns and making split-second trading decisions. They adapt to changing market conditions in real-time, optimizing trading strategies to maximize gains or minimize losses. The use of AI in algorithmic trading has led to greater efficiency and liquidity in financial markets, but also raises concerns such as increased market volatility and the potential for AI-driven market manipulations.

- **The Future of AI in Finance**: Looking ahead, the potential of AI in finance is vast and multi-faceted. Future advancements are expected to yield even more sophisticated AI models capable of deeper financial analysis and more accurate predictions. This could lead to further automation of financial processes, from customer service to compliance monitoring, and even more complex areas such as wealth management and financial planning. As AI technologies evolve, they are poised to enhance customer experiences significantly, offering more intuitive and responsive financial services. However, this also brings challenges like ensuring data privacy, managing ethical considerations, and adapting to regulatory changes. The intersection of AI with emerging technologies like blockchain could further revolutionize finance, creating more secure, transparent, and efficient financial systems. As AI continues to grow and integrate deeper into the financial sector, it holds the promise of shaping a more dynamic, inclusive, and innovative financial landscape.

As we conclude our exploration of AI in the financial sector, it's clear that AI is not just an emerging technology but a pivotal force driving innovation and efficiency in finance. This chapter has illuminated the myriad ways AI is being leveraged – from risk assessment to customer service enhancement – showcasing its profound impact on the industry. As we look to the future, the integration of AI in finance promises further advancements, underscoring the importance of embracing and adapting to this technological evolution in the world of finance.

Enhancing Blockchain with AI

In this insightful section of Chapter 2, we explore the dynamic intersection of blockchain technology and artificial intelligence (AI) in the realm of finance. This fusion of blockchain's secure, decentralized ledger with AI's analytical prowess and predictive capabilities opens up unprecedented possibilities. We'll delve into how this combination not only enhancing existing financial systems but also paving the way for innovative financial models and solutions.

- **Synergizing Blockchain and AI**: The integration of AI with blockchain technology creates a groundbreaking amalgamation that enhances the capabilities of both technologies. AI's advanced analytical and predictive capabilities, when combined with blockchain's immutable and transparent nature, open up new avenues for developing secure, intelligent, and self-regulating financial systems. This synergy allows for more sophisticated data analysis on blockchain networks, enabling better fraud detection, more efficient transaction processing, and enhanced security protocols. For instance, AI can analyze patterns within a blockchain to detect anomalous transactions that may indicate fraudulent activity, thereby increasing the security and integrity of the network.

- **Optimizing Blockchain Operations with AI**: AI plays a crucial role in enhancing the operational efficiency of blockchain networks. By applying machine learning algorithms, AI can effectively manage and analyze the large volumes of data within blockchain systems. This results in improved transaction processing speeds and enhanced scalability of the network. AI-driven predictive analysis can foresee network bottlenecks and optimize resource allocation to maintain optimal performance during peak times. For example, AI algorithms can anticipate high traffic on a blockchain network and automatically adjust the system to handle increased loads, thus ensuring consistent transaction speeds and reducing latency.

- **Smart Contracts Get Smarter with AI**: Smart contracts, one of the most innovative aspects of blockchain, are significantly enhanced with AI integration. AI enables smart contracts to execute more complex, conditional operations based on external data inputs. By integrating AI, smart contracts can analyze real-time data from external sources and make autonomous decisions. For example, an AI-enhanced smart contract in an insurance application could automatically adjust claim payouts based on real-time data such as weather conditions or market prices. This not only adds a layer of dynamic functionality to smart contracts but also opens up possibilities for their application in complex financial and business scenarios, such as dynamic pricing models, automated compliance checks, and more nuanced risk management strategies. The integration of AI into smart contracts represents a significant leap forward in automating and optimizing financial and business processes, heralding a new era of intelligent, responsive, and adaptive financial systems.

- **Predictive Analytics in Blockchain Markets**: AI's predictive analytics bring a revolutionary edge to blockchain markets, especially in cryptocurrency trading and DeFi sectors. By leveraging vast datasets, AI algorithms can analyze historical trends, market sentiments, and user behaviors within these decentralized networks. This allows AI systems to anticipate market movements, identify potential investment opportunities, and forecast future market trends with a high degree of accuracy. For instance, in cryptocurrency trading, AI can predict price fluctuations based on market indicators, social media sentiments, and global economic events. In DeFi, predictive analytics can assess the risk profiles of various assets, guide investment strategies, and optimize lending protocols based on evolving market dynamics. This level of predictive intelligence is invaluable for traders and investors seeking to make informed decisions in the highly volatile and dynamic blockchain markets.

- **Enhancing Security on the Blockchain**: AI's role in augmenting blockchain security is significant. The integration of AI with blockchain technology offers advanced monitoring capabilities. AI algorithms are designed to continuously scrutinize blockchain networks for anomalous patterns and potential security breaches. By analyzing transaction data in real-time, AI can identify abnormal patterns indicative of hacking attempts or fraudulent activities. This can include unusual transaction volumes, rapid changes in wallet balances, or suspicious network traffic. Upon detecting such anomalies, AI systems can initiate immediate responses, such as triggering alerts, isolating suspect transactions, or even temporarily halting network activities to prevent potential security breaches. This proactive security approach adds an extra layer of defense to the already robust blockchain infrastructure, making the network more resilient against cyber threats and attacks.

- **AI in Fraud Detection and Prevention**: AI's application in fraud detection within blockchain systems is a crucial advancement. These

AI systems utilize machine learning algorithms to analyze transaction patterns and identify irregularities that could signify fraudulent activities. By learning from historical data, AI models become increasingly proficient at recognizing the signatures of different types of fraud, such as double-spending, phishing attempts, or unauthorized access. When suspicious activity is detected, the AI system can take immediate action, including alerting network administrators, flagging transactions for review, or automatically implementing security protocols to mitigate the risk. This capacity for real-time fraud detection not only enhances the security of blockchain networks but also instills greater confidence among users and investors in the integrity and reliability of blockchain-based financial systems. The advanced fraud detection capabilities of AI are essential in maintaining the trust and stability of these emerging financial ecosystems.

- **Future Prospects of AI and Blockchain Integration**: The integration of AI and blockchain holds immense potential for future technological advancements. One promising innovation is the development of AI-driven consensus mechanisms, which could revolutionize how blockchain networks validate transactions and maintain security. These AI-based systems could adaptively analyze network conditions and optimize consensus protocols in real-time, enhancing efficiency and scalability. Another exciting prospect is the use of AI to enhance privacy features on blockchain networks. By employing advanced encryption techniques and intelligent data management protocols, AI could ensure even higher levels of data security and user privacy. Furthermore, the future might see the emergence of fully autonomous, AI-managed blockchain networks, where AI algorithms oversee network operations, optimize performance, and respond to evolving network demands without human intervention. These networks could self-regulate, adapt to changing environments, and potentially offer more sophisticated services such as automated regulatory compliance or real-time risk management.

- **Challenges and Considerations**: While the fusion of AI and blockchain presents significant opportunities, it also brings unique challenges. One of the primary challenges is the complexity inherent in integrating two advanced technologies. Each has its distinct architecture and operational dynamics, making their integration a sophisticated and nuanced process. Another crucial consideration is the ethical use of AI in financial transactions. As AI systems become more involved in financial decision-making, ensuring transparency, fairness, and accountability in these systems becomes paramount. There's also the challenge of maintaining blockchain's decentralized ethos in the face of powerful AI systems. As AI capabilities expand, there's a risk that these systems could centralize control or influence within blockchain networks, potentially undermining the decentralized principles that are foundational to blockchain technology. Addressing these challenges requires a careful and considered approach, balancing innovation with the core values and security aspects inherent to blockchain and AI.

As we wrap up this section, it's evident that the synergy between blockchain and AI is more than just a technological marvel; it's a transformative force in the financial sector. By integrating the robust security of blockchain with the smart analytics of AI, we're witnessing the birth of a new era in finance — one that is more secure, efficient, and intelligent. The implications of this fusion are far-reaching, promising a future where financial services are not only more reliable but also more attuned to the evolving needs of a digital world.

Case Studies of Blockchain and AI Integration

In this segment of Chapter 2, we turn our focus to real-world applications, diving into case studies that showcase the integration of blockchain and AI in finance. These examples will illustrate not just the theoretical possibilities, but the practical impacts and innovations that have been achieved. Through these case studies, we gain a deeper understanding of how blockchain and AI are being used to solve complex financial challenges and transform the industry.

- **AI-Driven Asset Management on the Blockchain**: A prominent example of AI-driven asset management on the blockchain is an innovative platform that leverages machine learning algorithms to dynamically adjust investment portfolios. This system analyzes vast amounts of market data, including price trends, trading volumes, and global economic indicators, to make predictive decisions about asset allocation. For instance, consider a blockchain-based platform that employs neural networks to recognize patterns in cryptocurrency markets, enabling it to anticipate price movements and adjust trading strategies in real-time. This approach allows for a more responsive and intelligent asset management system that can capitalize on market opportunities faster than traditional models.

- **AI-Enhanced Verification Processes for Transactions**: A practical application of AI in enhancing blockchain transaction verification is evident in a system designed for identity verification and fraud detection. Utilizing AI algorithms, this system scrutinizes each transaction for anomalies that could indicate fraudulent activity, such as unusual transaction sizes or patterns that deviate from a user's typical behavior. By integrating facial recognition and biometric verification, the system ensures the legitimacy of user identities, substantially minimizing the risk of identity theft and unauthorized transactions. A real-world example could be a blockchain-based banking platform that employs AI for real-time monitoring and verification, ensuring a high level of security and user trust in the system.

- **AI-Based Predictive Markets on Decentralized Platforms**: An innovative use of AI in predictive markets on decentralized platforms can be observed in a system where AI algorithms analyze diverse data sets, including financial news, market indicators, and even social media sentiment, to forecast market trends. This system can dynamically adapt to changing market conditions, offering predictions on asset prices, economic shifts, or even political events. For instance, a decentralized trading platform might use AI to predict cryptocurrency price movements, enabling traders to make informed decisions. The AI system continuously learns from market outcomes, refining its predictive models for greater accuracy. This integration not only enhances the predictive capacity of the markets but also introduces a level of efficiency and intelligence previously unattainable in traditional prediction models.

- **Blockchain and AI in Supply Chain Finance**: Consider a case study involving a global retail company implementing a blockchain and AI integrated system for its supply chain finance. The blockchain element offers a transparent and immutable record of each product's journey from manufacturer to consumer, enhancing traceability and accountability. Simultaneously, AI algorithms analyze historical supply chain data, providing predictive insights for inventory management. This includes anticipating demand spikes based on market trends or seasonal changes, and recommending inventory adjustments. For instance, the AI might predict a surge in demand for certain products based on social media trends and advise increasing stock levels, while the blockchain ensures accurate tracking of these inventory changes.

- **AI in Enhancing Blockchain Energy Efficiency**: Explore a case study of a blockchain network that employs AI to optimize its energy consumption. The primary concern addressed here is the high energy requirement of blockchain operations, especially in proof-of-work systems. AI algorithms can predict the most energy-efficient times to conduct mining activities and allocate resources accordingly. They can also identify patterns in transaction activities to suggest more energy-efficient ways of processing and validating transactions. An example might be a blockchain network that uses AI to dynamically adjust its mining difficulty and node activity, thereby reducing overall energy consumption without compromising network security or efficiency.

- **AI for Regulatory Compliance on Blockchain**: Present a case study of a financial institution that uses AI to navigate the complex regulatory environment of blockchain-based transactions. The AI system is programmed to understand and keep up-to-date with international financial regulations, including AML and know-your-customer (KYC) standards. It automatically screens transactions on the blockchain for potential regulatory violations, flagging suspicious activities for further investigation. This system could significantly reduce the time and resources required for compliance, ensuring that the institution's blockchain transactions are both efficient and legally compliant. For example, the AI might analyze patterns in transaction data to identify and report potential money laundering activities, a crucial capability in today's increasingly regulated financial landscape.

- **AI-Powered Risk Assessment in Decentralized Finance (DeFi)**: Explore a practical case study of AI's role in DeFi risk assessment. Focus on a DeFi platform that has integrated AI algorithms to assess and rate the risk associated with various DeFi projects and smart contracts. These AI systems analyze a multitude of factors, such as historical performance data, the developer's reputation, smart contract code integrity, and market trends, to generate risk profiles for different DeFi offerings. For instance, an AI algorithm might evaluate the likelihood of a smart contract being susceptible to certain types of cyber-attacks or identifying patterns that suggest a high risk of fraud. This level of assessment helps users make informed decisions about their investments and contributes to a safer DeFi ecosystem.

- **Conclusion and Future Outlook**: In summarizing these case studies, highlight the transformative impact AI and blockchain integration is having on the financial sector. Reflect on the potential this integration holds for creating more secure, efficient, and transparent financial systems. Look towards the future, considering advancements in AI like deep learning and predictive analytics, and blockchain innovations like scalability solutions and interoperable networks. Speculate on how these evolving technologies might further disrupt traditional financial models, democratize finance, and facilitate more equitable global economic participation. Conclude with a call to action for continued innovation and collaboration in this field, emphasizing the importance of responsible development and ethical considerations in this rapidly evolving space.

Concluding our journey through these enlightening case studies, we have observed firsthand how the integration of blockchain and AI is reshaping the financial landscape. From enhancing security to optimizing operations, these real-world examples provide a vivid glimpse into a future where technology drives financial innovation. As we move forward, these case studies serve as beacons, guiding the way for further advancements and inspiring continued exploration in the vast potential of blockchain and AI in finance.

Challenges and Limitations

In this critical part of Chapter 2, we address the challenges and limitations inherent in the rise of blockchain and AI in the finance sector. While these technologies offer transformative potential, it's essential to acknowledge and understand the hurdles they face, from technical constraints to ethical dilemmas. This section delves into these issues, offering a balanced perspective on the path forward for blockchain and AI in finance.

- **Scalability Issues**: The integration of blockchain and AI in finance is not without its scalability challenges. For blockchain, particularly those networks utilizing Proof of Work (PoW), there's a bottleneck in processing a high volume of transactions quickly. This limitation becomes more pronounced as the network grows. On the AI front, the requirement for extensive data processing can put a strain on blockchain networks. This scalability issue can lead to slower transaction speeds and increased costs, making it less viable for high-frequency trading or real-time financial analysis. Discuss possible solutions being explored, like the development of more efficient blockchain protocols (e.g., Proof of Stake) and the integration of off-chain solutions for AI data processing, which aim to enhance the scalability of these technologies while maintaining security and decentralization.

- **Complexity of Smart Contracts**: Smart contracts, while transformative, bring their own set of complexities and challenges. Their coding and execution need to be flawless, as even minor errors can lead to vulnerabilities, potentially leading to significant financial losses or security breaches. Highlight specific incidents where smart contract vulnerabilities have been exploited, leading to significant financial losses or breaches of trust. Discuss the efforts being made to improve the creation and testing of smart contracts, such as advanced programming languages specifically designed for blockchain, enhanced testing protocols, and the role of AI in identifying potential vulnerabilities in smart contracts before they are deployed.

- **Regulatory Challenges**: The rapid advancement of blockchain and AI technologies in finance is creating a gap in regulatory frameworks. These technologies often operate in a global, decentralized environment that traditional regulatory approaches are not equipped to handle. Explore the challenges regulators face, such as understanding the technical nuances of blockchain and AI, ensuring consumer protection in a largely unregulated space, and managing cross-border transactions that may fall under multiple jurisdictions. Highlight the tension between fostering innovation and protecting consumers, and the ongoing debate about how to regulate decentralized and semi-anonymous systems. Mention initiatives like regulatory sandboxes and international collaborations aimed at developing more comprehensive and adaptive regulatory frameworks for these emerging technologies.

- **Data Privacy and Security Concerns**: In the realm of finance, data privacy and security are of utmost importance. The integration of AI and blockchain poses unique challenges in this regard. Blockchain is known for its transparency, which can conflict with the privacy requirements of financial transactions. Simultaneously, AI systems require access to vast amounts of data, raising concerns about data privacy and protection. Explore how regulations like the General Data Protection Regulation (GDPR) impact the application of these technologies in the financial sector. Discuss the solutions being developed to address these challenges, such as private or permissioned blockchains that offer more controlled access, and the use of advanced encryption methods and data anonymization techniques in AI to enhance data privacy while still benefiting from AI's analytical capabilities.

- **Integration with Existing Financial Systems**: Integrating blockchain and AI technologies with legacy financial systems presents significant technical and institutional challenges. The technical aspect involves the compatibility of new, decentralized technologies with older, centralized systems. Address the technical hurdles such as data format standardization, system interoperability, and maintaining data integrity during the transition. On the institutional side, there's often resistance from established financial entities that may perceive these technologies as a threat to their existing business models and market positions. Discuss the initiatives and strategies being adopted to facilitate this integration, like collaborative projects between fintech startups and traditional banks, and the development of interoperable platforms that can bridge the gap between old and new systems.

- **Ethical Considerations in AI Usage**: The use of AI in finance brings forward several ethical considerations. One major concern is algorithmic bias - the risk that AI systems might perpetuate and even amplify existing biases present in their training data, leading to unfair or discriminatory financial decisions. Discuss the importance of ethical AI development practices, including the use of diverse and unbiased data sets, regular audits of AI systems for biased outcomes, and the implementation of ethical guidelines for AI development and deployment in financial contexts. Additionally, explore the ethical implications of allowing AI systems to make autonomous financial decisions, such as the potential for AI-driven speculation or market manipulation, and the need for clear accountability mechanisms when AI systems are used in financial decision-making.

- **Maintaining the Balance between Decentralization and Control**: One of the central challenges in integrating blockchain and AI in finance is preserving the decentralized nature of blockchain technology while leveraging the centralized, decision-making power of AI. This balance is crucial as blockchain's value proposition lies in its decentralization, which ensures transparency and reduces single points of failure, while AI's strength is in centralized data processing and decision-making capabilities. Discuss strategies to maintain this balance, such as developing decentralized AI models where decision-making processes are distributed across the network or creating hybrid models where AI assists in decision-making without compromising the decentralized nature of the blockchain. Explore the potential of emerging technologies like federated learning, which allows AI models to learn from decentralized data sources without needing to centralize the data, thus aligning with blockchain's ethos.

- **Conclusion and Looking Forward**: Conclude the chapter by reflecting on the intersection of blockchain and AI as a fertile ground for innovation in finance. While there are challenges, such as scalability, integration with existing systems, and maintaining a balance between decentralization and AI's centralized nature, these are not insurmountable. Emphasize the potential of ongoing innovation, collaborative efforts between technology developers, financial institutions, and regulators, and the development of thoughtful, forward-looking regulatory frameworks. Express optimism about the future, envisioning a financial landscape that is more efficient, secure, and inclusive, driven by the synergistic integration of blockchain and AI. Highlight the transformative potential these technologies hold for creating a financial ecosystem that is not only more responsive to the needs of its users but also more resilient and adaptable to future challenges and opportunities.

Having explored the various challenges and limitations facing blockchain and AI in finance, we emerge with a nuanced understanding of these revolutionary technologies. Despite their immense potential, the journey ahead is paved with complex obstacles that require careful navigation. This exploration not only highlights the need for continued innovation but also emphasizes the importance of addressing these challenges to fully harness the transformative power of blockchain and AI in the world of finance.

The Future Outlook of Blockchain and AI in Finance

As we venture into the concluding segment of Chapter 2, we cast our gaze forward to the future of blockchain and AI in finance. This section is dedicated to envisioning the potential trajectory and long-term impact of these groundbreaking technologies in reshaping the financial landscape. We'll explore predictions, emerging trends, and the possibilities that lie ahead, providing a roadmap for what the financial future might hold in this rapidly evolving digital era.

- **Emergence of Decentralized Finance (DeFi)**: DeFi, leveraging blockchain technology, is poised to significantly alter the financial sector. Its potential to democratize finance is immense, offering enhanced accessibility and a variety of financial products to a broader audience. AI could be instrumental in this transformation, enhancing security protocols on DeFi platforms, providing personalized financial products based on user data analysis, and enabling more efficient predictions in market trends and behaviors. The integration of AI in DeFi could lead to a more intuitive and user-friendly financial environment, breaking down traditional barriers to financial access and empowering users with more control over their financial transactions.

- **Tokenization of Real-World Assets**: The concept of tokenizing tangible assets like real estate, art, or commodities and converting them into digital tokens on a blockchain is gaining traction. This innovative approach, supported by AI's analytical prowess, can create more liquid markets, facilitate fractional ownership, and allow for more nuanced asset management. AI's role in assessing asset values, predicting market trends, and personalizing investment strategies could redefine asset trading and ownership, making it more accessible and versatile.

- **Advancements in AI-Powered Predictive Analytics**: The future of AI in finance is intricately linked to its ability to process and analyze vast datasets. With advancements in machine learning and data processing, AI's predictive analytics can offer unprecedented insights into market dynamics, risk assessment, and investment opportunities. The integration of AI with blockchain's secure and transparent infrastructure could further enhance the accuracy and reliability of these financial predictions, leading to more informed and strategic decision-making in finance.

- **Global Impact on Financial Inclusion**: Blockchain and AI have the potential to revolutionize financial inclusion on a global scale. These technologies can provide access to financial services for unbanked populations, especially through mobile platforms. The possibility of low-cost remittances, microloans, and affordable insurance products could significantly impact economic empowerment in developing regions. The integration of blockchain and AI promises to bridge the financial divide, offering secure and accessible financial services to those traditionally excluded from the financial system.

- **Integration of AI in Regulatory Compliance (RegTech)**: AI's role in regulatory technology (RegTech) could greatly streamline compliance processes. By automating transaction monitoring and ensuring adherence to international regulations, AI can significantly reduce the operational burden on financial institutions. This would not only make compliance more efficient but also more accurate, reducing the likelihood of regulatory violations and enhancing the overall integrity of the financial system.

- **Enhanced Personalization in Banking and Insurance**: The combination of AI and blockchain technology could usher in a new era of personalized financial services. AI's capacity to analyze individual customer data, coupled with the secure and transparent nature of blockchain, can enable highly tailored banking and insurance offerings. From custom financial advice based on individual spending habits and financial goals to personalized insurance packages that align with specific customer needs and risk profiles, the possibilities for customization are vast and varied.

- **Challenges and Ethical Considerations**: While the potential of blockchain and AI in finance is significant, it also presents challenges and ethical considerations. Key among these is ensuring robust cybersecurity measures to protect sensitive financial data. Additionally, concerns around data privacy and the ethical implications of AI-driven financial decision-making warrant careful consideration. The integration of these technologies must be approached with a focus on ethical standards and a commitment to protecting consumer rights and privacy.

- **Concluding Thoughts**: Concluding this chapter, it's clear that blockchain and AI hold transformative potential for the finance sector.

Their integration promises to make finance more efficient, secure, and inclusive. However, realizing this potential fully requires ongoing innovation, a collaborative approach involving tech and financial experts, and thoughtful regulation that fosters growth while safeguarding against risks. As we look to the future, the synergy between blockchain and AI stands as a beacon of innovation, holding the promise of reshaping the financial landscape for the better.

Concluding our journey through the dynamic realm of blockchain and AI in finance, we leave with a forward-looking perspective that merges optimism with realism. The future of these technologies in the financial sector is not just a matter of technological advancement but also of how we, as a society, choose to embrace and integrate them. As we close this chapter, it's clear that the road ahead is as promising as it is fraught with challenges, inviting continuous exploration, adaptation, and innovation in the fascinating intersection of technology and finance.

As we conclude Chapter 2, we are left with a profound understanding of the transformative role that blockchain and AI are playing in the financial sector. This chapter has taken us through the intricate workings of blockchain technology, highlighted its disruptive influence on financial transactions, and introduced the groundbreaking potential of AI in finance. We have seen how the integration of blockchain with AI is not just enhancing existing financial systems but is also paving the way for innovative financial solutions.

The real-world case studies and applications discussed in this chapter illustrate the tangible benefits these technologies offer, from increased efficiency and security to the democratization of financial services. Yet, the journey of blockchain and AI in finance is not devoid of challenges. As we have explored, issues like scalability, regulatory hurdles, and data privacy remain critical areas needing attention and creative solutions.

As you turn the page to Chapter 3, "The Promise of Decentralized Currencies," take a moment to reflect on the broader implications of blockchain and AI in our financial lives. Consider how these technologies could further evolve and integrate with decentralized currencies. What new opportunities could this convergence create? How might it address some of the challenges we've discussed? Chapter 3 will delve deeper into the world of decentralized currencies, exploring their potential to revolutionize our financial systems and the very concept of money.

Chapter 3
The Promise of Decentralized Currencies

In Chapter 3, we delve into the captivating world of decentralized currencies, exploring the transformative potential they hold. This segment is an odyssey into the heart of what makes decentralized currencies not just a financial innovation, but a radical shift in how we perceive and interact with money. Here, we unravel the core principles, benefits, and revolutionary promise that these currencies bring to the table, challenging the traditional paradigms of monetary exchange and financial autonomy.

Defining Decentralized Currencies

- **Fundamental Definition and Principles**: Decentralized currencies represent a paradigm shift in how currency is conceptualized and utilized. Unlike centralized financial systems governed by institutions like banks and governments, decentralized currencies operate on a peer-to-peer network. This network is built upon blockchain technology, where each transaction is recorded and verified by multiple nodes in the network, ensuring transparency and security. This decentralized nature fundamentally changes the dynamics of financial transactions, moving away from a system of centralized control to a more democratic, user-driven model.

- **The Role of Consensus Mechanisms**: Key to the functioning of decentralized currencies are consensus mechanisms like Proof of Work (PoW) and Proof of Stake (PoS). These mechanisms are critical for validating transactions and maintaining the currency's integrity and security. For example, PoW involves miners solving complex computational problems to validate transactions and secure the network, a process that is energy-intensive but crucial for the network's trustworthiness. On the other hand, PoS offers a less energy-intensive alternative, where validators are chosen based on the number of coins they hold and are willing to "stake" or lock up as collateral, promoting energy efficiency and faster transaction validation.

- **Distributed Ledger Technology (DLT)**: The core of decentralized currencies lies in DLT, which enables the secure and transparent recording of transactions. This technology ensures that every transaction is publicly recorded and immutable, making it nearly impossible to alter or delete past transactions. This level of transparency and security is a stark contrast to traditional financial systems, where records are centralized and more vulnerable to manipulation and unauthorized access.

- **Decentralization and Removal of Intermediaries**: Decentralized currencies revolutionize financial transactions by eliminating the need for traditional intermediaries like banks. This decentralization speeds up transactions and reduces costs, making financial services more accessible. It opens up financial opportunities for people in remote or underserved areas, who may not have access to traditional banking services, thereby bridging the financial inclusion gap.

- **Enhanced Security and Privacy**: Decentralized currencies offer superior security and privacy compared to traditional financial systems. The use of cryptographic techniques and the decentralized nature of blockchain technology make these currencies inherently resistant to cyber-attacks and fraud. Each transaction is securely encrypted, and the distributed nature of the blockchain makes it nearly impossible for hackers to compromise the data integrity.

- **Global Accessibility and Inclusivity**: Decentralized currencies are not bound by national borders or specific financial institutions, making them globally accessible. Anyone with an internet connection can participate in these financial networks, regardless of their location. This universal accessibility is a significant step towards financial inclusivity, offering people from all corners of the world the opportunity to engage in global financial transactions without the need for traditional banking infrastructure.

- **Control and Empowerment of Users**: In contrast to traditional currencies, where control is often in the hands of government entities and financial institutions, decentralized currencies empower individuals by giving them full control over their financial assets. Users have autonomy over their transactions, without the fear of censorship or seizure by central authorities. This empowerment is particularly impactful in regions with unstable currencies or restrictive financial policies, where decentralized currencies offer a stable and independent means of financial exchange.

- **Concluding Thoughts**: In summary, decentralized currencies are not just a new form of money; they represent a radical shift in the global financial paradigm. By democratizing access to capital, fostering financial inclusion, and challenging traditional dynamics of financial power, these currencies have the potential to reshape the global financial landscape. As we continue to explore their possibilities, it is clear that decentralized currencies hold immense potential for creating a more equitable and accessible financial future for all.

Evolution and Diversification of Decentralized Currencies

- **The Genesis - Bitcoin**: Bitcoin's inception in 2009 marked a monumental shift in digital currency. Conceived by the enigmatic Satoshi Nakamoto in response to the 2008 financial crisis, Bitcoin offered an innovative solution: a decentralized currency immune to governmental control or inflation. Its core technology, blockchain, was a public ledger system that facilitated transparent and secure transactions without the need for centralized authority, laying the foundation for the future of decentralized finance.

- **The Rise of Altcoins**: Bitcoin's groundbreaking success inspired the development of various alternative cryptocurrencies, known as altcoins. These digital currencies, including Ethereum, Litecoin, Ripple, and others, aimed to expand upon or offer distinct functionalities compared to Bitcoin. Ethereum, for example, introduced the concept of smart contracts, enabling not just transactions but programmable agreements and applications, broadening blockchain's scope beyond simple financial exchanges.

- **Introduction of Different Blockchain Protocols**: The diversity of blockchain protocols forms the backbone of the cryptocurrency ecosystem. Bitcoin's blockchain was the first, but soon Ethereum introduced a different protocol designed for more extensive use cases, like decentralized applications (dApps). These protocols vary in their approaches to issues such as transaction speed, overall network security, and scalability, significantly influencing the performance and use cases of the respective cryptocurrencies.

- **Consensus Models – Beyond Proof of Work**: The landscape of consensus models in blockchain has evolved to address various challenges. Bitcoin's PoW model, while secure, is energy-intensive. In response, newer models like PoS and DPoS emerged, offering more energy-efficient and scalable solutions. Cryptocurrencies like Ethereum are transitioning to these new models to address environmental concerns and improve transaction efficiency.

- **The Emergence of Tokens and ICOs**: The rise of Ethereum's ERC-20 token standard revolutionized the digital currency space by facilitating the creation of Initial Coin Offerings (ICOs). These tokens, different from traditional cryptocurrencies, often represent assets or utilities within specific platforms or projects, broadening the scope of blockchain applications and attracting diverse investor interest.

- **Diversification into Niche Markets**: The diversification of decentralized currencies has given rise to niche-market cryptocurrencies. Privacy-focused coins like Monero and Zcash offer enhanced anonymity, while others like VeChain target specific sectors, such as supply chain management, showcasing the adaptability and sector-specific applications of blockchain technology.

- **Challenges with Diversity**: While the diversification of decentralized currencies fosters innovation, it also introduces challenges like market fragmentation. Users face complexity in navigating different cryptocurrencies, each with its unique features and functionalities. Additionally, the issue of interoperability arises, with the need for seamless interaction between various blockchain systems becoming increasingly important.

- **Conclusion and Future Perspective**: The evolution of decentralized currencies has been rapid and transformative. Looking ahead, the potential for further innovation is immense, with trends like the integration of AI in blockchain and the development of interoperability solutions shaping the future landscape. Regulatory developments will also play a critical role in shaping this dynamic and evolving ecosystem, as the world adapts to the growing impact and potential of decentralized currencies.

Economic Empowerment Through Decentralization

- **Financial Inclusion for the Unbanked**: Decentralized currencies are pivotal in bridging the financial divide. Globally, a significant portion of the population lacks access to traditional banking, either due to geographical remoteness or economic constraints. Decentralized currencies bypass these barriers, offering services like microloans, savings, and remittances via simple mobile applications. This access is transformative, enabling individuals in even the most remote areas to participate in the global economy.

- **Reducing Reliance on Traditional Banking Systems**: Traditional banking systems are often laden with high fees and complex requirements, creating barriers to financial freedom. Decentralized currencies dismantle these barriers, offering a streamlined and cost-effective alternative. Without the need for intermediaries, users gain autonomy over their financial transactions, free from the constraints of traditional banking infrastructures.

- **Facilitating Peer-to-Peer Transactions**: The peer-to-peer nature of decentralized currencies fundamentally changes how individuals transact. By eliminating intermediaries, these transactions become more direct and efficient, significantly reducing costs. For instance, a craftsman in a developing country can directly sell goods to international buyers, receiving payments in cryptocurrency without exorbitant transaction fees or delays.

- **Empowering Micro-Entrepreneurs and Small Businesses**: Decentralized currencies level the playing field for small businesses and micro-entrepreneurs. By facilitating access to global markets and easing the process of cross-border transactions, these currencies enable smaller entities to compete on a larger scale. They bypass traditional barriers to entry, such as bank credit requirements and international transaction hurdles, fostering entrepreneurial growth and innovation.

- **Enhanced Control Over Personal Finances**: In regions where local currencies are volatile or subject to strict controls, decentralized currencies offer a stable and autonomous alternative. Individuals can safeguard their savings against hyperinflation, engage in global trade, or invest in digital assets, all while maintaining control over their financial destiny.

- **Supporting Community-Driven Financial Initiatives**: Decentralized currencies have the power to fuel community-based financial initiatives. Through crowdfunding and community investment programs, these currencies enable collective financing of local projects, from infrastructural developments to social enterprises, fostering a sense of community autonomy and empowerment.

- **Addressing Economic Disparities**: The decentralized nature of these currencies holds the potential to redistribute economic power. They challenge the traditional financial hierarchy, offering a more equitable system where access to financial resources and opportunities isn't limited by socio-economic status, geographic location, or institutional barriers.

- **Conclusion – A Vision for Inclusive Economics**: In conclusion, decentralized currencies herald a new era of inclusive economics. They offer a framework for a more equitable financial landscape, where access to financial services is a universal right, not a privilege. The ongoing evolution in this field promises further innovation, but responsible use and regulation are essential to ensure these technologies benefit the broader society, reducing economic disparities and enhancing global economic participation.

Decentralization and Enhanced Security

- **Fundamentals of Cryptographic Security**: Decentralized currencies rely heavily on cryptographic methods for security. The most fundamental of these is public and private key cryptography, where a public key is used to generate wallet addresses and a private key is used to sign transactions, ensuring that only the owner can spend their funds. This dual-key system provides a robust layer of security, as the public key alone cannot be used to derive the private key. It ensures that transactions on a blockchain are both secure against unauthorized access and verifiable by anyone.

- **Resilience Against Fraud and Cyber Attacks**: The resilience of decentralized currencies against fraud and cyber-attacks stems from their distributed ledger technology. Each transaction is recorded on multiple nodes across the network, creating a ledger that is virtually tamper-proof. This distributed nature makes it extremely challenging for a single entity to alter transaction data. As a result, blockchain networks like Bitcoin and Ethereum provide a level of security that is typically unattainable in centralized systems.

- **Trustless Transactions**: In blockchain technology, 'trustless' doesn't mean a lack of trust, but rather the ability to transact without needing to trust the counterparty or an intermediary. This is made possible by the blockchain's transparency and immutability; once a transaction is recorded, it cannot be altered. This system ensures that all parties can trust the network's mechanics without needing to trust each other, significantly reducing the possibility of fraud.

- **Security in Smart Contracts**: Smart contracts, self-executing contracts with the terms directly written into code, are a critical feature of many decentralized platforms. They automatically execute and enforce agreements when predefined conditions are met, without human intervention. These contracts, when designed with rigorous security standards, minimize risks associated with manual processing and subjective interpretation, thus enhancing the overall security of the platform.

- **Preventing Double Spending**: A key challenge in digital currencies is preventing the same unit of currency from being spent more than once. Decentralized currencies address this through the blockchain, which keeps a time-stamped record of every transaction. This ledger is constantly verified by network nodes, ensuring that each digital token or coin is unique and cannot be duplicated or spent twice.

- **User Empowerment in Security**: Decentralized currencies empower users by giving them full control over their assets through private keys. Unlike traditional banking systems, where third parties have custody of financial assets, blockchain technology enables users to have complete ownership. This means they are responsible for their own asset security, including safeguarding their private keys, which are the only way to access their funds.

- **Challenges and Future Developments in Security**: Despite the robust security of decentralized systems, challenges persist, such as the secure management of private keys and potential vulnerabilities in smart contract code. Future developments are likely to include more user-friendly key management solutions and advanced cryptographic techniques, like quantum-resistant algorithms, to stay ahead of evolving cyber threats.

- **Conclusion – The Security Advantage**: Decentralized currencies offer a revolutionary approach to financial security. Moving from a system that relies on trust in centralized entities to a trustless, blockchain-based system marks a significant shift. This new paradigm enhances the security of financial transactions, reduces the risk of fraud and cyber-attacks, and empowers users with control over their own assets, setting the stage for a more secure and transparent financial future.

Impact on Global Financial Systems

- **Disruption of Traditional Financial Models**: Decentralized currencies are upending traditional financial models by facilitating direct peer-to-peer transactions without intermediaries like banks. This shift is significant as it redefines the role of financial institutions, which have traditionally been central to all monetary transactions. Decentralized Finance (DeFi) platforms exemplify this change by offering services like lending, borrowing, and investing outside the traditional banking system, thereby democratizing access to financial services.

- **Influence on Monetary Policies**: Decentralized currencies pose a unique challenge to governmental monetary policies. Operating independently of central banks, these currencies dilute the efficacy of conventional tools like interest rate adjustments and money supply controls. The decentralized nature of these currencies makes them difficult to regulate, posing a conundrum for central banks aiming to maintain financial stability and monitor monetary flows.

- **Challenge to Fiat Currency Dominance**: The increasing acceptance of decentralized currencies signals a potential shift in the dominance of fiat currencies. In economies plagued by instability or hyperinflation, decentralized currencies offer an alternative, more stable store of value. This could lead to scenarios where these currencies are preferred for savings and transactions, challenging the traditional supremacy of fiat money.

- **Facilitating Cross-Border Transactions**: Decentralized currencies streamline cross-border transactions by eliminating the need for currency exchange and traditional international transfer processes. This simplification and cost reduction make global trade and remittances more efficient, directly benefiting businesses and individuals who regularly engage in international transactions.

- **Encouraging Financial Innovation**: The emergence of decentralized currencies is a catalyst for innovation in the financial sector. Traditional financial institutions are increasingly exploring blockchain technology and even developing their digital currencies to remain relevant and competitive in this evolving landscape.

- **Potential for a More Inclusive Financial System**: Decentralized currencies hold the promise of a more inclusive financial system. By providing access to financial services for the unbanked and underbanked populations, these currencies could play a pivotal role in reducing global economic disparities and fostering financial inclusion.

- **Challenges and Risks**: Despite their potential, decentralized currencies come with inherent challenges and risks. Their volatility can be a deterrent for widespread adoption. Regulatory uncertainty remains a significant hurdle, and the potential for their use in illegal activities raises concerns. These issues represent significant challenges to their full integration into the global financial system.

- **Conclusion – A Paradigm Shift in Finance**: Decentralized currencies represent a paradigm shift in the global financial landscape. Their ability to drive innovation, challenge existing financial models, and offer a more inclusive and efficient system underscores their transformative potential. As these currencies continue to evolve, they could reshape the very foundations of how global finance operates.

Case Studies of Decentralized Currency Adoption

- **Remittances in Developing Countries**: In Zimbabwe and Venezuela, decentralized currencies have become vital in facilitating remittances. With traditional banking systems unstable and remittance fees high, cryptocurrencies like Bitcoin provide a more stable and cost-effective way to receive money from abroad. In Zimbabwe, where hyperinflation has eroded the value of local currency, Bitcoin offers a more reliable store of value. In Venezuela, amidst economic sanctions and currency devaluation, cryptocurrencies have become a crucial means for families to receive financial support from relatives overseas, thereby supporting local economies and individual financial stability.

- **Online Marketplaces and E-Commerce**: Online marketplaces such as Overstock and Newegg have embraced decentralized currencies, accepting Bitcoin and other cryptocurrencies. This integration caters to a global customer base, offering a borderless and efficient payment option that reduces transaction fees. These platforms exemplify how e-commerce can leverage decentralized currencies to provide more inclusive payment methods, making it easier for international customers to shop online without the complexities of currency exchange.

- **National Cryptocurrency Experiments**: Venezuela's introduction of the 'Petro', a national cryptocurrency, represents an attempt to circumvent international sanctions and economic challenges. This initiative aims to provide an alternative to the traditional financial system but faces challenges, including international acceptance and technological infrastructure. The Petro's case illustrates the complexities and potential of national-level cryptocurrency initiatives, especially in countries facing economic sanctions or monetary instability.

- **Decentralized Currencies in Crisis Situations**: During Greece's financial crisis, cryptocurrencies like Bitcoin emerged as an alternative to the strained local banking system. As banks imposed capital controls and fears of monetary devaluation grew, Greeks turned to Bitcoin for financial security and autonomy. This shift highlighted cryptocurrencies' role as a safe haven during economic instability, offering an alternative to traditional financial systems in times of crisis.

- **Blockchain-based Aid and Donations**: The United Nations World Food Programme's use of Ethereum blockchain to aid Syrian refugees is a notable case study. This initiative utilized blockchain technology to distribute aid efficiently and transparently, reducing the risk of fraud and ensuring that aid reached its intended recipients. This approach revolutionized humanitarian aid, demonstrating blockchain's potential to enhance transparency and efficiency in aid distribution.

- **Small Businesses Embracing Decentralized Currencies**: Small businesses around the world are increasingly adopting decentralized currencies, recognizing their benefits in reducing transaction fees and accessing a global customer base. For instance, a café in Berlin accepting Bitcoin has seen increased patronage from cryptocurrency enthusiasts worldwide. This global reach, combined with lower transaction costs, enables small businesses to compete in a broader market.

- **Tourism and Cryptocurrency**: In the tourism industry, several establishments have started accepting cryptocurrencies as payment, catering to the needs of international travelers. Hotels in Switzerland, for example, accept Bitcoin, simplifying transactions for guests and reducing currency exchange hassles. This adoption showcases how decentralized currencies can enhance the convenience of international travel and transactions.

- **Conclusion – Real Impact and Growing Adoption**: These case studies underscore the real-world impact and growing adoption of decentralized currencies across various sectors. From facilitating remittances in economically challenged countries to revolutionizing e-commerce and aid distribution, decentralized currencies demonstrate practical utility and transformative potential. Their increasing acceptance in diverse global contexts highlights their role in shaping a more inclusive and efficient financial future.

Challenges and Criticisms of Decentralized Currencies

- **Price Volatility**: Decentralized currencies like Bitcoin and Ethereum are known for their significant price volatility. This aspect poses a risk for investors and users, as the value of these currencies can fluctuate wildly in short periods. For example, Bitcoin experienced a rapid price increase in late 2017, reaching nearly $20,000, only to fall sharply in the following year. Such volatility can lead to substantial financial gains or losses, affecting individual holders' investment decisions and impacting the broader financial market, including influencing investor sentiment and market stability.

- **Regulatory Challenges**: The regulatory landscape for cryptocurrencies is fragmented and varies significantly across different countries. While some countries like Japan have embraced cryptocurrencies with open regulation, others like China have imposed strict controls or outright bans. The absence of a standardized global regulatory framework creates a complex environment for compliance, affecting the legal status and mainstream financial institutions' adoption of cryptocurrencies. This lack of uniformity leads to legal uncertainties, hampers global transactions involving cryptocurrencies, and potentially stifles innovation in this sector.

- **Environmental Concerns**: Certain cryptocurrencies, particularly those using Proof of Work (PoW) consensus mechanisms like Bitcoin, are criticized for their high energy consumption. The Bitcoin network, for example, consumes more electricity annually than some countries. This environmental impact has led to growing calls for more sustainable practices in the cryptocurrency industry. In response, there is a shift towards adopting less energy-intensive consensus mechanisms, such as Proof of Stake (PoS), which significantly reduce the energy requirement for validating transactions and maintaining the network.

- **Debate on Long-Term Viability**: The debate on the long-term viability of decentralized currencies centers around their scalability, mass adoption, and integration into the existing financial ecosystem. Critics argue that scalability issues, fluctuating values, and regulatory uncertainties might hinder their widespread adoption. Proponents, however, believe that continuous technological advancements and increasing global interest could lead to their eventual integration as mainstream financial instruments.

- **Dependence on Technology and Infrastructure**: Decentralized currencies heavily rely on technology and infrastructure, such as stable power grids and internet connectivity. In regions with unreliable power or limited internet access, this reliance can be a significant drawback. For instance, a power outage could prevent access to digital wallets, while a weak internet connection might delay or disrupt transactions, posing challenges to the practical use of cryptocurrencies in these areas.

- **Security Risks and Fraud**: Despite the inherent security features of blockchain technology, the cryptocurrency sector is not immune to risks such as exchange hacks, phishing scams, and wallet thefts. Notable incidents, like the Mt. Gox hack where a large amount of Bitcoin was stolen, highlight the importance of robust cybersecurity measures and the need for individuals to practice vigilant digital asset management to safeguard their investments.

- **Impact on Traditional Financial Systems and Employment**: The rise of decentralized currencies could potentially disrupt traditional financial systems and affect employment within the banking and financial services sectors. If there is a large-scale shift towards decentralized currencies, it could lead to a restructuring of the banking industry, possibly affecting jobs in areas like transaction processing and financial advisory services. This shift might also spur the development of new job roles focused on blockchain and cryptocurrency technologies.

- **Conclusion – Navigating the Challenges**: In concluding, it's essential to recognize both the challenges and the criticisms faced by decentralized currencies, as well as the ongoing efforts to address these issues. The field requires informed decision-making by investors, thoughtful and adaptable regulatory approaches by governments, and continuous innovation by technology developers. The future of decentralized currencies will likely be shaped by a collaborative effort among various stakeholders, aiming to balance innovation with stability and security.

As we close Chapter 3, it's clear that the world of decentralized currencies is not just a fleeting trend, but a significant shift in the financial paradigm. These currencies bring with them a promise of democratizing finance, offering greater accessibility, and challenging traditional banking models.

The case studies and examples we've explored underscore their potential to reshape economies, empower individuals, and foster global financial inclusion.

However, the journey of decentralized currencies is not without its hurdles. The challenges of volatility, regulatory uncertainties, and environmental concerns loom large, presenting complex problems that require innovative solutions. As we move into a future where technology increasingly intersects with finance, the role of decentralized currencies will undoubtedly continue to evolve and spark debate.

As we transition to Chapter 4, "The Power of Decentralization and AI," consider the implications of combining decentralized financial systems with the cutting-edge capabilities of artificial intelligence. How might this synergy further revolutionize our approach to money, transactions, and financial services? What new possibilities and challenges could emerge from this fusion? The next chapter delves into these questions, exploring the transformative potential of AI in the realm of decentralized finance.

As we conclude Chapter 3, we step back to reflect on the profound implications of decentralized currencies. Their emergence isn't merely a blip in the financial timeline but a seismic shift that heralds a new era of monetary freedom and empowerment. We leave this chapter with a deeper appreciation of how decentralized currencies are redefining the boundaries of financial systems and democratizing economic power, encouraging us to embrace and participate in this exciting journey towards a more inclusive and decentralized financial future.

Chapter 4
The Power of Decentralization and AI

Chapter 4 opens the doors to a realm where the forces of decentralization and artificial intelligence converge, reshaping the financial landscape. This chapter is dedicated to exploring how the synergy between these two powerful technologies is unlocking unprecedented possibilities. From enhancing security and efficiency to enabling more personalized financial services, we journey through the myriad ways in which this fusion is not just innovating but revolutionizing the way financial operations are conducted and experienced.

Breaking Down Centralized Control

- **The Fundamentals of Decentralization**: Decentralization is a core principle in the world of digital currencies, distinguishing them from traditional financial systems. Unlike centralized currencies issued by governments and regulated by central banks, decentralized currencies operate on a distributed ledger, such as blockchain. This technology allows for the creation, distribution, and management of currency without a central authority. This system distributes financial control across a network of computers, each participating in the validation and recording of transactions, thus democratizing financial operations and reducing the central point of failure.

- **Shift in Power Dynamics**: The advent of decentralized digital currencies heralds a significant shift in financial power dynamics. Traditionally, financial power has been concentrated in the hands of central banks and financial institutions, which control monetary policy and financial transactions. In contrast, decentralized systems distribute this power across their networks, giving individual users more control. For instance, Bitcoin's blockchain technology allows users to transact directly without intermediaries, challenging traditional banking models and reshaping the financial landscape.

- **Financial Autonomy and Freedom**: Decentralization grants individuals unprecedented financial autonomy and freedom. In a decentralized system, users have complete control over their digital assets and can conduct transactions directly with others. This direct control leads to benefits such as lower transaction fees, faster processing times, and greater privacy. For example, in countries with stringent financial controls or unstable currencies, citizens have turned to cryptocurrencies like Bitcoin to preserve their wealth and transact freely beyond government restrictions.

- **Impact on Traditional Banking and Government Control**: Decentralized digital currencies pose a significant challenge to traditional banking systems and government monetary control. They operate independently of the financial policies and regulations typically imposed by governments, potentially diminishing the influence of central banks. This independence raises questions about how monetary policy might be shaped in the future and what role central banks might play in a world where digital currencies are widely adopted.

- **Decentralized Decision-Making**: In decentralized financial systems, decision-making is often a collective process involving the network's participants. Unlike centralized systems where decisions are made by a single entity, decentralized networks rely on consensus mechanisms, like Proof of Work or Proof of Stake, where changes to the network or protocol are agreed upon by the majority of its participants. This democratic approach to decision-making ensures that changes are beneficial for the majority and not influenced by a single controlling party.

- **Resilience Against Censorship and Control**: One of the key strengths of decentralized systems is their resilience against censorship and external control. The distributed nature of blockchain technology means there's no central authority that can unilaterally block transactions or censor specific users. This makes decentralized currencies particularly appealing in regions with strict financial censorship or where freedom of transaction is limited.

- **Potential Challenges and Critiques**: Despite the advantages, decentralization comes with its own set of challenges and critiques. Security concerns, such as the risk of 51% attacks on smaller networks, are significant. Moreover, the digital divide means not everyone has equal access to these technologies. Additionally, the anonymity provided by decentralized systems can be exploited for illicit activities, raising concerns about their use in money laundering or financing illegal activities.

- **Conclusion – A Paradigm Shift**: Decentralization in the world of digital currencies represents a fundamental shift in the financial sector, moving away from traditional, centralized financial systems towards a more democratized model. This shift promises increased autonomy and efficiency but also brings new challenges in security, regulation, and equitable access. As this technology continues to evolve, it is reshaping the very fabric of the financial world, requiring users, regulators, and governments to adapt to its transformative impact.

AI as a Catalyst in Decentralized Systems

- **Enhancing Blockchain Capabilities with AI**: Artificial Intelligence (AI) significantly enhances blockchain technology by optimizing its performance. AI algorithms are adept at analyzing vast amounts of blockchain data to improve transaction speed and network efficiency. For instance, AI can detect and respond to potential security threats in real time, enhancing the overall security of blockchain networks. A practical example is the use of AI in identifying irregular patterns that could signal a security breach, thereby proactively safeguarding the blockchain against cyber threats.

- **Optimizing Transaction Processes**: AI revolutionizes transaction processing in decentralized systems by efficiently managing network loads and optimizing transaction fees. By predicting periods of high network congestion, AI algorithms can adjust transaction fees dynamically, ensuring that users don't overpay during times of low activity. Moreover, AI can enhance cross-border transactions by predicting and optimizing exchange rates in real-time, significantly reducing the cost and time involved in international transfers.

- **Improving Smart Contract Functionality**: AI plays a crucial role in improving the functionality of smart contracts in decentralized systems. It automates the verification of contract conditions, reducing reliance on manual checks and minimizing human error. For example, AI-powered systems can audit smart contracts to identify vulnerabilities or flaws, ensuring their reliability and efficiency. This application of AI not only boosts the confidence in smart contract technology but also expands its potential use cases across various sectors.

- **Enabling Efficient Decentralized Applications (DApps)**: AI contributes significantly to the development of sophisticated and user-friendly decentralized applications (DApps). By integrating AI-driven user interfaces and predictive analytics, DApps become more intuitive and engaging for users. This integration is crucial in making DApps accessible to a wider audience, thereby fostering broader adoption of decentralized technologies.

- **AI in Fraud Detection and Security**: AI is instrumental in enhancing the security of decentralized systems through advanced fraud detection capabilities. Machine learning algorithms, with their ability to analyze transaction patterns, are adept at identifying anomalies that could indicate fraudulent activity. This proactive approach to security is essential in protecting users' assets and maintaining the integrity of decentralized networks.

- **Personalization in DeFi Services**: AI enables a high degree of personalization in decentralized finance (DeFi) services. By analyzing individual transaction histories and preferences, AI algorithms can tailor financial products and services to meet specific user needs. This personalization enhances user experience, making DeFi more accessible and appealing to a diverse user base.

- **Potential Challenges and Ethical Considerations**: Integrating AI into decentralized systems brings its own set of challenges and ethical considerations. Concerns about data privacy and the potential for AI bias are paramount. There is a need for transparent and accountable AI systems, especially in the context of financial decisions that can have significant implications for users. Ensuring ethical use of AI in decentralized finance is critical for maintaining user trust and the system's integrity.

- **Conclusion – The Synergy of AI and Decentralization**: The integration of AI and decentralized systems represents a synergistic relationship that enhances the capabilities of both technologies. AI not only improves the technical aspects of decentralized finance but also introduces a level of personalization and efficiency previously unattainable. This synergy holds the promise of redefining the future landscape of finance, making it more secure, efficient, and user-friendly. The potential for innovation in this space is vast, signaling an exciting future for the intersection of AI and decentralized financial technologies.

AI-Driven Risk Management and Fraud Detection

- **Principles of AI in Risk Management**: AI's role in risk management within decentralized finance (DeFi) is pivotal. By processing vast volumes of transaction data, AI algorithms identify patterns and trends that human analysts might overlook. These systems can analyze historical market behavior and current market conditions to forecast potential risks. This capability is crucial in a landscape where market dynamics are constantly evolving, allowing for a proactive approach to risk management.

- **Enhancing Security with AI**: AI algorithms significantly enhance the security of decentralized systems. Machine learning models are adept at detecting unusual transaction patterns, a key indicator of potential fraudulent activities. By continuously learning and adapting to new data, these models stay ahead of sophisticated fraud techniques, thus bolstering the overall security of the DeFi platforms. This involves analyzing transaction frequency, size, and origin to flag anomalies that deviate from typical user behavior, acting as an early warning system against potential security breaches.

- **Real-Time Risk Assessment**: AI plays a crucial role in real-time risk assessment, offering instant evaluations of transaction risks. These assessments are based on a variety of factors, including market volatility, transaction history, and current market conditions. By processing these complex variables in real-time, AI systems provide users and platforms with immediate risk evaluations, enabling informed decision-making and timely intervention to mitigate potential losses.

- **Fraud Detection in Action**: AI's effectiveness in fraud detection is evident in various case studies within the crypto space. For example, AI systems have been instrumental in identifying and halting large-scale phishing attacks and unauthorized access attempts. These systems analyze transaction patterns and flag discrepancies, such as unusually large withdrawals or transfers to known suspicious wallets, thereby preventing substantial financial losses and maintaining the integrity of the platform.

- **Mitigating Risks in DeFi**: In the DeFi sector, AI addresses unique challenges like liquidity management, loan underwriting, and optimizing yield farming strategies. AI tools assess the risk profile of loans by analyzing borrowers' transaction histories and current market conditions, ensuring that lending is both profitable and secure. Similarly, in yield farming, AI algorithms can predict market movements to suggest the most lucrative and least risky farming strategies, thus maximizing returns while minimizing exposure.

- **Ethical Considerations and Transparency**: The use of AI for risk management and fraud detection in DeFi must adhere to ethical standards and transparency. It's essential to address and mitigate any inherent biases in AI algorithms to avoid unfair treatment of users. Moreover, the decisions made by these AI systems need to be transparent and explainable to ensure user trust and regulatory compliance.

- **Future Prospects and Innovations**: The future of AI in risk management and fraud detection is promising, with advancements in deep learning and neural networks poised to further enhance these systems. These advanced AI models could provide even more accurate predictions and identify sophisticated fraud patterns, staying ahead of increasingly complex financial crimes in the DeFi space.

- **Conclusion – Balancing Innovation with Security**: The integration of AI in DeFi represents a critical balance between embracing innovation and ensuring robust security. AI-driven risk management and fraud detection are key to maintaining this equilibrium. These technologies foster trust among users and regulators alike, promoting the continued growth and maturation of the DeFi ecosystem. As DeFi evolves, the role of AI in safeguarding and optimizing these platforms will become increasingly vital, marking a new era of secure and efficient digital finance.

Personalization and AI in Financial Services

- **The Era of Personalized Finance**: AI has ushered in an era of personalized finance, revolutionizing the sector by tailoring services to individual needs. Unlike traditional finance's generalized approach, AI leverages user data to offer customized solutions. This paradigm shift is marked by AI's ability to analyze spending habits, investment history, and personal financial goals, thereby delivering a more nuanced and user-centric financial experience.

- **Customized Investment Advice**: AI's impact is particularly profound in investment advice. By analyzing market trends, individual risk tolerance, and personal investment goals, AI platforms can offer bespoke investment strategies. Robo-advisors, for example, utilize AI algorithms to craft personalized investment portfolios, adjusting recommendations in real-time based on market fluctuations and individual user profiles.

- **AI-Driven Customized Risk Assessment**: In risk assessment, AI transcends the limitations of traditional credit scoring by evaluating a broader range of financial behaviors and personal data. Machine learning models consider a user's transaction history, spending patterns, and even lifestyle choices to provide a more comprehensive risk profile. This nuanced approach allows for more precise and fair assessment, particularly beneficial for those with limited credit history.

- **Tailoring Financial Products**: In decentralized finance, AI is instrumental in creating financial products that cater to individual circumstances. It designs loan packages, insurance policies, and savings accounts that align with specific user profiles, considering factors like risk tolerance, financial goals, and income stability. This personalization ensures that financial products are more relevant, accessible, and beneficial to each user.

- **Enhancing User Experience with AI**: AI significantly enhances user experience in financial services. AI-driven chatbots provide real-time assistance, while personalized alerts and recommendations keep users informed and engaged. These interactive and responsive tools make navigating financial platforms more intuitive, encouraging greater user interaction and satisfaction.

- **Challenges in Personalization**: Personalization in finance is not without challenges. Privacy concerns top the list, as AI relies heavily on personal data. The accuracy of AI predictions and the ethical use of data also pose significant challenges. Safeguarding user data and ensuring transparent, ethical AI practices are crucial for maintaining user trust and the integrity of financial services.

- **Future of AI in Personalized Finance**: The future of AI in personalized finance is promising, with potential advancements like behavioral finance algorithms and integration with IoT, offering even more nuanced financial services. This could lead to dynamic financial products that adapt in real-time to user behavior and changing financial landscapes, pushing the boundaries of personalized financial solutions.

- **Conclusion – A New Frontier in Finance**: AI-driven personalization marks a new frontier in finance. It democratizes access to financial services, making them more tailored and efficient for individual needs. While it represents a significant leap forward, the journey must be navigated with responsibility and a focus on user protection. The balance between innovation and ethical considerations will be key in shaping this exciting future of finance.

AI's Role in Regulatory Compliance and Monitoring

- **AI in Regulatory Adaptation**: AI's prowess in adapting to the dynamic regulatory landscape of decentralized finance is pivotal. AI algorithms are uniquely designed to update in real-time, reflecting the latest regulatory changes. This ability ensures that decentralized platforms remain compliant with evolving global financial regulations, including those related to anti-money laundering (AML) and know your customer (KYC) standards. By integrating these adaptive algorithms, decentralized platforms can navigate the complexities of regulatory compliance with unprecedented agility.

- **Monitoring Transactions for Compliance**: AI systems excel in monitoring transactions across decentralized networks. They analyze vast volumes of transaction data, identifying patterns that may indicate regulatory breaches. By flagging unusual activities or transactions that deviate from established norms, these AI systems play a critical role in enforcing compliance with key regulatory frameworks, thereby safeguarding the integrity of decentralized financial platforms.

- **Automating Reporting Processes**: AI dramatically streamlines regulatory reporting in decentralized finance. By automating the collection and analysis of financial data, AI ensures that reports are comprehensive, accurate, and timely. This automation reduces the administrative burden and minimizes the risk of human error, ensuring that decentralized platforms meet their regulatory reporting obligations efficiently.

- **Auditing in a Decentralized Environment**: In decentralized environments, AI is redefining the auditing process. AI algorithms can swiftly and thoroughly scrutinize blockchain transactions, detecting irregularities or inconsistencies that may elude manual audits. This capability not only enhances the accuracy of audits but also boosts the overall trust in decentralized financial systems.

- **Evolving Regulations and AI Responsiveness**: The rapidly evolving regulatory landscape presents a significant challenge in decentralized finance. AI's responsiveness to these changes is crucial. By continuously learning and adapting, AI systems can help platforms navigate complex and shifting regulatory requirements, ensuring ongoing compliance and reducing the risk of inadvertent breaches.

- **Ethical Considerations and Transparency**: The use of AI in regulatory compliance raises important ethical considerations. It's imperative that AI systems operate transparently, especially when making decisions that could impact users' financial activities. Ensuring these systems are free from biases and respect user privacy is essential to maintain trust and uphold ethical standards in decentralized finance.

- **The Future of Regulatory AI Technologies**: Looking ahead, AI technologies are poised to further advance regulatory compliance. Future innovations might include predictive regulatory compliance capabilities, where AI not only responds to existing regulations but also anticipates potential future changes. Such proactive compliance could greatly enhance the efficiency and effectiveness of regulatory adherence in decentralized finance.

- **Conclusion – AI as a Regulatory Partner**: In conclusion, AI emerges as an indispensable regulatory partner in decentralized finance. Its capabilities in monitoring, reporting, and adapting to regulatory changes are fundamental to maintaining the legitimacy and integrity of decentralized platforms. By enabling compliance with global financial standards, AI ensures that decentralized finance remains a secure, trustworthy, and viable component of the global financial ecosystem.

Predictive Analytics and Market Insights

- **Unveiling AI's Predictive Power**: The role of AI in predictive analytics within decentralized finance is revolutionary. By analyzing historical data and current market trends, AI can forecast future market movements with remarkable accuracy. This capability is particularly valuable in the volatile realm of digital currencies, where market dynamics change rapidly. AI's predictive power aids in navigating these complexities, offering critical insights for informed decision-making.

- **Market Forecasting and Trend Analysis**: AI excels in processing and analyzing vast amounts of financial data from decentralized platforms. It employs sophisticated algorithms to identify market patterns and trends that might be imperceptible to human analysts. This deep analysis provides valuable insights into market movements, revealing potential investment opportunities and aiding in comprehensive risk assessment.

- **Enhancing Investment Strategies**: AI-driven predictive analytics is a game-changer for investment strategies in decentralized finance. Investors leverage AI to sift through market data, identifying profitable opportunities and assessing investment risks. This data-driven approach enables investors to make informed decisions that align with their investment objectives, optimizing their financial strategies in the volatile crypto market.

- **Real-Time Market Insights**: AI's capacity to provide real-time market insights is crucial in the fast-paced environment of decentralized finance. It processes data from diverse sources, including social media, news feeds, and economic indicators, offering a holistic view of market sentiments. This instantaneous analysis allows investors to react swiftly and strategically to market fluctuations.

- **Behavioral Economics and AI**: Incorporating behavioral economics, AI sheds light on investor behavior patterns and market psychology. It analyzes how market sentiment and investor actions impact price movements, offering a nuanced understanding of market dynamics. This integration of psychology and finance through AI helps in predicting market trends more accurately.

- **AI in Risk Management**: Predictive analytics is vital in risk management within decentralized finance. AI algorithms can anticipate market risks and vulnerabilities, enabling investors and platforms to proactively mitigate potential threats. This foresight is essential in maintaining the stability and integrity of investments in the decentralized market.

- **Challenges and Ethical Considerations**: The application of AI in predictive analytics is not without challenges and ethical concerns. Issues like data privacy, the reliability of AI predictions, and potential biases in AI models need careful consideration. Establishing transparent and ethical guidelines is paramount to ensure the responsible use of AI in financial analytics.

- **The Future of AI in Market Prediction**: Looking ahead, advancements in AI technology promise to enhance its predictive capabilities further. Innovations such as quantum computing could revolutionize AI's ability to process complex data sets, making it an indispensable tool in strategic financial planning. The future of decentralized finance could see AI becoming integral to market prediction and decision-making processes.

- **Conclusion – Navigating the Future with AI**: AI's predictive analytics marks a transformative shift in decentralized finance. Its ability to provide comprehensive market insights and foresight is creating a new era of strategic decision-making. As we navigate the evolving landscape of decentralized finance, AI stands as a pivotal tool, guiding investors and stakeholders through its complexities with informed and data-driven insights.

Future Scenarios of AI-Enhanced Decentralized Finance

- **AI's Evolutionary Path in Decentralized Finance**: As AI continues to evolve, its role in decentralized finance (DeFi) is poised for significant expansion. Future developments are likely to see AI technologies becoming more sophisticated and deeply integrated into DeFi systems. This integration could transform how financial operations are conducted, from automated trading to complex decision-making processes, making DeFi more efficient, responsive, and user-friendly.

- **Advanced Predictive Models**: The potential of AI to develop advanced predictive models in DeFi is enormous. These models could leverage large datasets, including historical market trends and real-time transaction data, to provide highly accurate forecasts. Such advancements could revolutionize investment strategies, offering unparalleled insights into market opportunities and risks, thereby aiding investors in making more informed decisions.

- **Autonomous Financial Management**: The future may hold AI systems capable of autonomously managing financial portfolios. These systems would make investment decisions based on a mix of market data, investor profiles, and predefined objectives. The real-time processing capabilities of AI could enable dynamic portfolio adjustments, optimizing for market conditions and individual risk tolerance.

- **AI and Personalized Financial Products**: AI's potential to personalize financial products in DeFi is vast. Future AI systems could design products that adapt to individual financial goals and changing market conditions. This personalization could extend to various financial services, including tailored investment options, customized insurance packages, and personalized loan offerings.

- **AI in Regulatory Innovation**: AI could play a pivotal role in regulatory innovation within DeFi. Future AI systems might not only adapt to existing regulatory frameworks but also proactively respond to emerging regulatory challenges. This proactive approach could ensure that DeFi platforms remain compliant, even as financial regulations evolve.

- **Decentralized AI Governance Models**: The concept of decentralized AI governance models in finance is intriguing. Such models could see AI not just assisting with financial operations but also contributing to the governance of DeFi platforms. AI could help in decision-making processes, policy formation, and maintaining the overall integrity of the platform, promoting efficiency and transparency.

- **Quantum Computing and AI**: The advent of quantum computing could significantly boost AI's capabilities in DeFi. Quantum computing's immense processing power could enable AI to solve complex financial problems faster and more accurately than ever before. This leap in capability could lead to groundbreaking advances in predictive analytics and problem-solving in the DeFi space.

- **Ethical and Security Implications**: As AI becomes more powerful within DeFi, addressing ethical and security implications becomes crucial. Ensuring robust security measures to protect against potential AI vulnerabilities and establishing ethical guidelines for AI use are paramount to harness its power responsibly and maintain public trust.

- **Interactive AI and Human Collaboration**: The future might see a collaborative relationship between AI and human intelligence in decentralized finance. This synergy could enhance creativity, adaptability, and resilience in financial decision-making, with AI providing data-driven insights and humans contributing nuanced understanding and ethical considerations.

- **Conclusion - A New Financial Horizon**: The convergence of AI and decentralized finance is shaping a new financial horizon. This synergy promises a transformative impact, redefining how finance is conducted and experienced. It holds the potential to make financial systems more inclusive, efficient, and aligned with individual needs, marking a significant shift in the global financial landscape.

As we conclude Chapter 4, it's evident that the amalgamation of decentralization and Artificial Intelligence is not just a fleeting trend but a formidable force shaping the future of finance. This synergy heralds a paradigm shift, ushering in an era where financial empowerment, efficiency, and innovation are not just ideals but tangible realities.

The journey through this chapter reveals how decentralization challenges traditional financial structures, redistributing power and control from centralized institutions to a more democratized, peer-to-peer network. This shift paves the way for enhanced financial autonomy, greater resistance to censorship, and a reimagining of financial services that are more inclusive and accessible.

Simultaneously, AI emerges as a catalyst, supercharging decentralized systems with its predictive prowess, risk management capabilities, and personalized financial solutions. AI's role in regulatory compliance and fraud detection is particularly noteworthy, positioning it as an indispensable ally in maintaining the integrity and legitimacy of decentralized financial systems.

As we look towards the horizon, the potential of AI and decentralization working in concert appears limitless. From advanced predictive analytics to autonomous financial management and ethical AI governance, the future beckons with promises of more dynamic, responsive, and inclusive financial ecosystems.

However, this journey is not without its challenges. The integration of AI and decentralization demands a thoughtful approach, balancing innovation with ethical considerations, security, and the essence of decentralization. The path forward requires a collaborative effort among technologists, regulators, and financial experts to navigate these challenges effectively.

In essence, Chapter 4 lays the groundwork for understanding the transformative impact of AI and decentralization in finance. It invites us to envision a future where financial systems are not just tools for economic transactions but enablers of a more equitable and empowered society. As we turn the page, the anticipation of what lies ahead in this exciting convergence of technology and finance is both exhilarating and inspiring.

Chapter 5
Accessibility and Efficiency
in Decentralized Systems

Chapter 5 delves into the heart of decentralized systems, focusing on their accessibility and efficiency. This exploration seeks to unravel how these systems democratize financial services, making them more accessible to a broader audience while enhancing the efficiency of transactions. We'll examine the mechanisms that allow for seamless, inclusive participation and the streamlined processes that mark the superiority of decentralized systems over traditional financial structures.

Bridging the Financial Divide with Decentralization

- **Understanding the Global Financial Divide:** The current global financial landscape is characterized by stark inequality. Millions across the world, especially in developing regions, find themselves excluded from basic banking and financial services. This exclusion is more than a mere inconvenience; it impedes individuals' ability to save, invest, and even participate in the broader economy, perpetuating cycles of poverty and limiting economic growth. The ripple effects of this divide are profound, affecting not just individuals but entire communities.

- **Decentralization as a Solution:** Decentralized financial systems offer a promising solution to this divide. By operating independently of traditional banking infrastructures, these systems make financial services accessible to anyone with internet access. Decentralized platforms are not bound by geographic limitations or the need for physical banking infrastructure, which often excludes rural or underprivileged areas.

- **Empowering the Unbanked:** The impact of decentralized finance (DeFi) on the unbanked is transformative. For instance, in parts of

Africa and Southeast Asia, DeFi platforms have enabled access to financial services previously unreachable. These platforms offer an array of services, from basic transactions to more complex financial operations like lending and borrowing, all without the need for traditional bank accounts.

- **Mobile Technology and Financial Inclusion:** Mobile technology is a crucial component in leveraging decentralized systems for financial inclusion. In many developing countries, where traditional banking infrastructure is sparse, smartphones have become ubiquitous. This widespread adoption of mobile technology allows decentralized applications (dApps) to reach a broad audience, offering financial services directly on users' mobile devices.

- **Lowering Barriers to Entry:** Decentralized systems significantly lower the barriers to financial services. Unlike traditional banking, which often requires extensive documentation, credit history, and sometimes even a minimum balance, decentralized platforms are much more accessible. They often require little more than a basic digital wallet, making them a viable option for those traditionally excluded from the financial system.

- **Case Studies of Impactful Projects:** Various projects demonstrate the potential of decentralized systems in enhancing financial inclusion. For example, in Kenya, blockchain-based microloan platforms have empowered local entrepreneurs by providing accessible, low-interest loans. Similarly, in the Philippines, cryptocurrency payment systems have enabled seamless and low-cost remittances, a crucial income source for many families.

- **Challenges and Potential Solutions:** Despite their potential, decentralized systems face challenges in bridging the financial divide. Issues such as inconsistent internet access, limited technological literacy, and varied regulatory landscapes pose significant hurdles. Solutions include developing more user-friendly interfaces, increasing local awareness and education about these technologies, and working with governments to create supportive regulatory frameworks.

- **Future Prospects for Financial Equality:** Looking ahead, decentralized systems hold immense promise in fostering financial equality. With ongoing advancements in blockchain technology and fintech, these systems could become even more accessible and efficient. The future could see a world where financial services are not a privilege but a readily available resource for all, driving global economic growth and personal financial empowerment.

Decentralization as a Tool for Financial Inclusion

- **Mobile-Based Cryptocurrency Wallets:** Mobile technology has fundamentally altered the landscape of financial access, especially in regions with limited banking infrastructure. Mobile-based cryptocurrency wallets are at the forefront of this change, providing a pivotal tool for financial inclusion. These wallets transform smartphones into digital banks, allowing users to securely store, send, and receive digital currencies. This technology bridges the gap for those who previously had no access to banking services, enabling them to participate in the global economy directly from their phones.

- **Decentralized Lending Platforms:** The rise of decentralized lending platforms marks a significant shift in how individuals and small businesses access capital. These platforms leverage smart contracts and blockchain technology to facilitate loans without traditional intermediaries like banks. This reduces costs, streamlines the process, and notably expands access to credit. For example, in regions like Sub-Saharan Africa, these platforms have empowered small-scale entrepreneurs with much-needed capital, fostering local economic growth and empowerment.

- **Blockchain-Based Remittance Services:** Remittances play a crucial role in the economies of many developing countries. Blockchain-based remittance services are revolutionizing this sector by offering solutions that are markedly faster, cheaper, and more transparent than traditional methods. These services significantly reduce the transaction fees, which are often a burden for migrant workers sending money home, and ensure that funds are transferred swiftly and securely.

- **Tokenization of Assets:** Decentralized systems are transforming the investment landscape through the tokenization of assets. This process allows for fractional ownership of assets like real estate or art, traditionally reserved for the affluent. Tokenization democratizes investment opportunities, enabling individuals with limited capital to invest in high-value assets, thus broadening economic participation and opportunity.

- **Crowdfunding and DAOs (Decentralized Autonomous Organizations):** Crowdfunding on decentralized platforms, particularly through DAOs, is redefining how projects receive financial backing. DAOs represent a shift towards community-driven finance, where individuals collectively make decisions and fund projects. This model has been instrumental in supporting various initiatives, from tech startups to social causes, bypassing traditional funding barriers.

- **Financial Education and Decentralized Systems:** Financial literacy is crucial for leveraging decentralized financial services effectively. Educational initiatives play a key role in teaching the unbanked and underbanked how to navigate digital currencies and engage with decentralized finance. Such programs are essential in ensuring that the benefits of decentralized finance are accessible and understandable to all, particularly in regions where financial education has been historically lacking.

- **Regulatory Challenges and Solutions:** The decentralized finance sector faces a complex regulatory landscape. The lack of uniform regulations across different jurisdictions poses challenges to its widespread adoption. Establishing clear and supportive regulatory frameworks is critical for these services to achieve their potential in enhancing financial inclusion. Discussions and collaborations among global regulators, fintech innovators, and financial institutions are essential in shaping policies that support the growth and safe use of decentralized financial services.

- **Future Innovations and Accessibility:** The future of financial inclusion through decentralized systems is promising, driven by continuous technological advancements. Future innovations in blockchain and decentralized finance are expected to further reduce barriers, making financial services even more accessible. This could include the development of more user-friendly platforms, integration with other emerging technologies like AI, and enhanced security features. These advancements hold the potential to make financial services not just accessible but also equitable and efficient for people worldwide, ushering in a new era of economic empowerment and global participation.

Improving Transaction Efficiency in Decentralized Finance

- **Rapid Transaction Processing:** Decentralized finance (DeFi) systems bring a remarkable improvement in transaction speed compared to traditional banking. Thanks to blockchain technology's distributed ledger, transactions in DeFi can be processed and verified almost instantaneously. This eliminates the multi-day waiting periods often experienced in conventional banking, transforming financial transactions into a matter of minutes or even seconds.

- **Elimination of Intermediaries:** A key feature of decentralized systems is the absence of traditional financial intermediaries such as banks and clearinghouses. This not only expedites the transaction process but also significantly reduces associated costs. Without these middlemen, processes like fund transfers and payments become direct and more streamlined, effectively cutting down on processing fees and service charges that typically inflate transaction costs.

- **Smart Contracts in Transaction Efficiency:** Smart contracts play a pivotal role in enhancing the efficiency of financial processes within DeFi. These digital contracts, encoded with predefined rules, execute transactions automatically once conditions are met. This automation eliminates the delays and errors associated with manual processing, thereby ensuring transactions are executed both swiftly and accurately.

- **Cross-Border Transactions:** DeFi has a transformative impact on cross-border transactions. It enables seamless global transactions by bypassing common barriers like currency exchange rates, international banking regulations, and traditional banking intermediaries. This revolutionizes international trade and finance, making it more accessible, faster, and less cumbersome for businesses and individuals alike.

- **Reduction in Transaction Costs:** The decentralized architecture of blockchain significantly lowers various transaction-related expenses. By cutting out intermediaries, reducing processing time, and lessening the reliance on physical infrastructure, blockchain technology delivers cost-effective transaction solutions, passing on these savings directly to users.

- **Challenges in Transaction Efficiency:** Despite its advantages, DeFi faces certain challenges that impact transaction efficiency. These include issues like network congestion, which can slow down transaction times, and scalability concerns that limit the number of transactions that can be processed simultaneously. Additionally, the energy efficiency of some blockchain protocols, particularly those relying on Proof of Work (PoW), remains a concern.

- **Innovations Enhancing Efficiency:** The DeFi space is continuously evolving, with innovations aimed at overcoming current inefficiencies. Developments such as layer 2 scaling solutions, which process transactions off the main blockchain, sharding techniques that divide the blockchain into smaller, more manageable parts, and new consensus mechanisms, are all aimed at resolving scalability and efficiency issues.

- **The Future of Transaction Efficiency in DeFi:** Looking ahead, the trajectory for transaction efficiency in decentralized finance is promising. Emerging technologies and ongoing research are likely to further enhance the speed and reduce the costs of transactions. Innovations such as quantum computing and more advanced blockchain protocols could revolutionize transaction processing, leading to an even more efficient, cost-effective, and rapid financial ecosystem. This future scenario paints an optimistic picture of DeFi's role in shaping a more agile and accessible financial world.

Cost Reduction in Financial Transactions

- **Overview of Traditional Banking Fees:** Traditional banking systems involve a range of fees, serving as a significant revenue source for banks. These include transfer fees for moving funds, foreign exchange fees for currency conversion, account maintenance fees for managing accounts, and more. These fees are structured based on transaction types, account types, and other banking services, reflecting the operational and administrative costs incurred by banks.

- **Decentralized Systems and Fee Elimination:** Decentralized systems, particularly those based on blockchain technology, offer a paradigm shift in the fee structure. By removing intermediaries such as banks and clearinghouses, these systems significantly reduce or even eliminate many common fees. The decentralized nature of blockchain transactions means that users often only pay minimal network fees, which are a fraction of the costs in traditional banking.

- **Comparison of Transaction Costs:** Comparing transaction costs in traditional and decentralized systems reveals a stark contrast. For example, international remittances through traditional banks can incur high fees and currency conversion costs, whereas blockchain-based transfers often involve much lower fees. Real-world case studies, such as using cryptocurrencies for remittances, demonstrate substantial cost savings for users.

- **Impact on Foreign Exchange Transactions:** Decentralized systems have a notable impact on foreign exchange transactions. Using cryptocurrencies for cross-border payments eliminates the need for currency exchanges, bypassing the associated fees and unfavorable exchange rates typically seen in traditional banking.

- **Reduced Overhead Costs:** Blockchain's decentralized nature significantly reduces the overhead costs typically associated with financial institutions. With less need for physical infrastructure and a reduced workforce for transaction processing, these savings can be passed to consumers in the form of lower transaction fees.

- **Challenges in Decentralized Fee Structures:** Despite the advantages, decentralized fee structures face challenges, such as fluctuating fees during periods of network congestion. Various blockchain networks are actively working on solutions to stabilize and optimize fee structures, ensuring affordability and consistency for users.

- **Innovations Leading to Further Cost Reductions:** The blockchain field is rife with innovations aimed at reducing transaction costs. Developments like off-chain transactions, which process transactions away from the main blockchain, and second-layer solutions like the Lightning Network for Bitcoin, are examples of efforts to minimize fees. More efficient consensus mechanisms are also being explored to enhance cost-effectiveness.

- **Long-term Implications for Consumers and Businesses:** The ongoing reduction in transaction costs in decentralized finance has significant implications. For consumers, it means more affordable access to financial services. For businesses, especially those engaged in international trade, the cost savings can be substantial. This trend towards lower costs could challenge traditional banking models, potentially leading to a more inclusive and efficient financial landscape where financial services are accessible to a broader segment of the population.

Microfinance and Decentralized Solutions

- **Introduction to Microfinance in Traditional Settings:** Microfinance traditionally aims to provide small loans, savings, and other financial services to those without access to traditional banking, primarily in developing economies. It plays a pivotal role in poverty alleviation by enabling low-income individuals to start small businesses, but faces challenges like high operational costs, and limited reach due to the reliance on physical infrastructure.

- **Blockchain Technology in Microfinance:** The integration of blockchain technology in microfinance is introducing significant improvements. Blockchain's inherent features like enhanced security, transparency, and lower transaction costs align well with the needs of microfinance. These features enable more secure and transparent handling of microtransactions and reduce costs associated with traditional microfinance models.

- **Case Studies of Blockchain in Microfinance:** Real-world applications of blockchain in microfinance illustrate its potential. For instance, initiatives in parts of Africa and Asia have successfully used blockchain for distributing microloans and managing micro-savings. These projects demonstrate how blockchain can streamline operations and reach previously underserved populations.

- **Reducing Operational Costs and Risks:** Decentralized finance offers notable cost reductions in microfinance operations. By minimizing the need for physical branches and extensive paperwork, blockchain significantly cuts down administrative overhead. This reduction in operational costs allows microfinance institutions to offer loans at lower interest rates, making financial services more affordable.

- **Improving Accessibility and Financial Inclusion:** Blockchain-based platforms are extending financial services to remote and underserved areas. These platforms enable individuals to access microloans and savings products directly through digital channels, bypassing the need for traditional banking systems and physical documentation, thus fostering greater financial inclusion.

- **Challenges and Limitations in Decentralized Microfinance:** While promising, blockchain application in microfinance is not without challenges. Technological barriers, such as limited digital literacy and lack of access to necessary devices, pose significant hurdles. Additionally, regulatory frameworks for blockchain and cryptocurrencies are still evolving, which could impact the deployment of these technologies in microfinance.

- **Innovations and Future Potential in Decentralized Microfinance:** The future of decentralized microfinance is bright, with ongoing innovations. Smart contracts, for example, are automating the loan disbursement and repayment processes, while cryptocurrencies are enabling microtransactions with lower fees. These advancements could further streamline microfinance services and expand their reach.

- **Impact Assessment and Ethical Considerations:** Evaluating the impact of decentralized microfinance involves considering both its benefits and risks. It's crucial to ensure that these technologies are used ethically and that they genuinely contribute to economic empowerment without exploiting users. Considerations should include fair access to services and protecting users from potential financial risks.

- **Concluding Thoughts on Decentralized Microfinance:** In conclusion, decentralized finance holds significant promise for transforming the microfinance sector. It can empower small entrepreneurs and contribute to economic growth in low-income areas. As this field evolves, it's essential to consider how blockchain can be further leveraged to promote sustainable development and reduce global financial disparities.

Challenges in Accessibility and Practical Solutions

- **Identifying Accessibility Challenges in Decentralized Systems:** The accessibility of decentralized finance is often hindered by various challenges. These include technological complexities, digital literacy gaps, inadequate infrastructure, and unclear regulatory frameworks. Such hurdles can prevent the widespread adoption and effective use of decentralized financial services.

- **Technological Barriers and User-Friendly Solutions:** Technological barriers, like the need for stable internet and advanced hardware, are significant. To overcome these, developing user-friendly interfaces that simplify complex processes is crucial. Creating lightweight applications compatible with basic hardware and limited internet can also enhance accessibility.

- **Bridging the Digital Literacy Gap:** Digital literacy is a key factor in using decentralized services. Initiatives for enhancing digital literacy, such as educational programs and community training, are vital. Platforms should be designed to be intuitive, minimizing the need for advanced technical knowledge.

- **Regulatory Hurdles and Collaborative Frameworks:** Navigating the regulatory landscape is challenging. Collaborative efforts between regulators, industry experts, and the community can lead to the development of clear and supportive regulations. This collaboration is essential for fostering innovation while ensuring user protection.

- **Infrastructure Development for Global Reach:** Strengthening infrastructure, particularly in remote and undeveloped regions, is essential for decentralized finance. Collaborations with local governments and international bodies can improve technological infrastructure, supporting the broader adoption of decentralized systems.

- **Inclusion of Diverse Populations:** Including diverse populations in the decentralized finance ecosystem is crucial. Tailoring financial products to various communities, ensuring language accessibility, and respecting cultural nuances can promote inclusivity and wider adoption.

- **Ongoing Innovations to Improve Accessibility:** Continuous technological advancements are key to improving accessibility. Innovations like mobile payment integration, satellite internet, and decentralized identity systems can make decentralized finance more accessible and user-friendly.

- **The Role of Community and Network Building:** Building a strong community and network is vital in enhancing accessibility. Peer-to-peer learning, community support systems, and partnerships between decentralized finance projects and local communities can create a more inclusive and supportive ecosystem.

- **Concluding Remarks on Overcoming Accessibility Challenges:** In conclusion, decentralized finance has the potential to revolutionize global finance, but realizing this potential requires addressing accessibility challenges. Collective efforts are needed to ensure that decentralized finance's benefits are available to everyone, irrespective of location, economic background, or technical ability. These efforts will pave the way for a more inclusive and equitable financial future.

Case Studies of Decentralization Impacting Lives

- **Empowerment Through Decentralized Microloans:** In a rural community in Kenya, a blockchain-based microloan platform has revolutionized access to capital. Small entrepreneurs, particularly women, have been able to secure loans without traditional collateral requirements. The story of Amina, who expanded her small farm and diversified her crops thanks to these accessible loans, underscores the transformative power of decentralized finance in driving economic growth at the grassroots level.

- **Decentralized Solutions in Crisis Situations:** In Venezuela, amid economic collapse and hyperinflation, decentralized finance has provided a crucial alternative. Cryptocurrencies have enabled citizens to preserve their savings and engage in transactions despite the local currency's plummeting value. This case study highlights how decentralized systems offer financial stability and access during times of crisis.

- **Financial Inclusion for the Unbanked:** In rural India, a village that lacked access to traditional banking services has been transformed by decentralized finance. Blockchain-based platforms have allowed villagers to securely save and transfer funds, opening up opportunities for small-scale investments and financial growth. Stories like Raj's, who started a small business with his savings, illustrate the life-changing impact of financial inclusion.

- **Decentralized Finance in Agriculture:** In Colombia, blockchain technology has enabled coffee farmers to achieve supply chain transparency, ensuring fair compensation and direct access to global markets. This case study showcases how decentralized finance can empower farmers, leading to increased profits and sustainable farming practices.

- **Crowdfunding Through Decentralization:** A decentralized crowdfunding platform helped a startup in the Philippines raise capital for an innovative clean energy project. This case reflects how decentralized finance can democratize funding, allowing entrepreneurs worldwide to connect with a global audience for financial support.

- **Remittance Revolution with Cryptocurrency:** The story of Maria, a Filipino nurse working in Canada, highlights the benefits of cryptocurrency remittances. By using a blockchain platform for sending money back home, she has significantly reduced transaction costs and time, greatly benefiting her family in the Philippines.

- **Blockchain for Educational Opportunities:** In Ghana, a blockchain platform has facilitated micro-scholarships for students from low-income families. This initiative has enabled students like Kwame to pursue higher education, offering a pathway to improved employment prospects and economic mobility.

- **Peer-to-Peer Energy Trading:** In a community in Australia, residents are using blockchain for peer-to-peer energy trading. Households with solar panels sell excess energy to neighbors, reducing costs and promoting the use of sustainable energy sources. This system has fostered a sense of community while contributing to environmental sustainability.

- **Concluding Thoughts on Decentralized Finance Impact:** These case studies collectively underscore the profound impact of decentralized finance on individuals and communities. From providing economic opportunities to enhancing sustainability, decentralized systems are proving to be powerful tools for building a more inclusive and equitable financial world. This transformative potential, illustrated through diverse real-world examples, offers a glimpse into a future where finance is more accessible, fair, and connected to the needs of communities globally.

Concluding Chapter 5, we have journeyed through the intricate pathways that make decentralized systems both accessible and efficient. This exploration has shed light on the transformative power of these systems in breaking down barriers and streamlining financial processes. As we progress, it becomes increasingly clear that the future of finance lies in systems that not only promise security and transparency but also ensure that financial empowerment is accessible to all, setting a new standard for efficiency in the global financial landscape.

Chapter 6
Understanding CBDCs

In Chapter 6, we embark on a comprehensive journey to understand Central Bank Digital Currencies (CBDCs). This chapter will dissect the concept, design, and potential implications of CBDCs in the evolving world of digital finance. From their role in national economies to their impact on global financial systems, we will explore how CBDCs could reshape traditional banking and monetary policies, offering a unique juxtaposition to decentralized digital currencies.

Fundamentals of Central Bank Digital Currencies (CBDCs)

- **Defining CBDCs:** Central Bank Digital Currencies (CBDCs) represent a significant innovation in the financial world. They are digital or virtual currencies issued and regulated by central banks, combining the trust and authority of traditional financial systems with the efficiency and agility of modern digital technology. CBDCs symbolize the digitization of national currencies, reflecting the evolving nature of money in an increasingly digital global economy.

- **Wholesale vs. Retail CBDCs:** It's crucial to distinguish between wholesale and retail CBDCs. Wholesale CBDCs are designed for and limited to financial institutions, primarily used for streamlining interbank settlements and other large-scale, financial operations. In contrast, retail CBDCs are aimed at the general public, akin to a digital form of cash, facilitating everyday transactions and offering a high-security alternative to physical currency.

- **Technological Infrastructure:** The technological infrastructure of CBDCs often involves blockchain or similar distributed ledger technologies (DLTs). However, unlike decentralized cryptocurrencies, CBDCs may operate on permissioned ledgers controlled by central authorities. This approach allows for greater regulation and stability while leveraging blockchain's efficiency and transparency. The choice between permissioned and permissionless systems reflects each central bank's priorities between control, privacy, and openness.

- **Motivations for CBDC Development:** Various factors motivate central banks to explore CBDCs. These include enhancing the efficiency and security of payments, fostering financial inclusion by reaching unbanked populations, retaining control over national monetary systems amidst the rise of private cryptocurrencies, and leveraging digital technology to streamline monetary policies.

- **Global Overview and Case Studies:** The global landscape of CBDC development is diverse. For instance, China's digital yuan is already in advanced trial phases, aiming to boost domestic and cross-border trade efficiency. In contrast, the Bahamas' Sand Dollar focuses on increasing financial inclusion in its archipelagic state. These case studies reveal different motivations and approaches to CBDC implementation.

- **CBDCs and Monetary Policy:** CBDCs could revolutionize monetary policy implementation. With programmable capabilities, they offer the potential for more direct and efficient policy applications, such as targeted fiscal stimulus or negative interest rates. This could lead to more precise control over money supply and greater transparency in policy execution.

- **Advantages of CBDCs:** CBDCs promise several benefits, including faster and cheaper transactions, reduced operational costs for banks, and the minimization of counterfeiting and financial crimes. They also offer enhanced traceability of funds, which can significantly improve the efficiency and security of financial transactions on a national and global scale.

- **Challenges and Concerns:** Despite their potential, CBDCs raise several concerns. Privacy issues are at the forefront, especially regarding how transaction data is used and protected. Cybersecurity is another major concern, given the digital nature of these currencies. Additionally, the integration of CBDCs into existing financial ecosystems poses technical and logistical challenges, with potential impacts on banking sector dynamics.

- **Interactive Element:** To engage readers further, consider posing thought-provoking questions like: "How might the introduction of a CBDC change your daily financial transactions?" or "What concerns would you have about using a digital currency issued by a central bank?" These questions encourage readers to reflect on the practical and personal impacts of CBDCs, fostering a deeper understanding of their potential role in the financial landscape.

Technological Infrastructure of CBDCs

- **Foundational Technology Choices:** The technological foundation of Central Bank Digital Currencies (CBDCs) hinges on two primary choices: traditional databases and blockchain technology. Traditional databases offer centralized control and proven reliability, making them a familiar choice for many central banks. In contrast, blockchain technology, underpinning many cryptocurrencies, provides decentralization, transparency, and enhanced security. The choice between these technologies reflects a central bank's priorities regarding control, transparency, and innovation.

- **Blockchain-Based CBDCs:** Several CBDC projects are exploring blockchain or Distributed Ledger Technology (DLT). This approach offers several advantages, including enhanced security against tampering, transparency in transactions, and the capacity to implement smart contracts for automated and programmable financial operations. Countries like Sweden and the Bahamas are experimenting with blockchain-based CBDCs, aiming to leverage these benefits while navigating the unique challenges of blockchain technology.

- **Traditional Database Approach:** Some central banks opt for traditional databases for their CBDCs due to the greater control and scalability they offer. Traditional databases can handle high transaction volumes more efficiently and align more closely with existing financial systems and regulations. This approach is often seen as a more pragmatic and less disruptive option, especially for economies with robust existing banking infrastructures.

- **Hybrid Models:** Recognizing the strengths and limitations of both blockchain and traditional databases, some central banks are considering hybrid models for their CBDCs. These models aim to blend the control and scalability of traditional databases with the transparency and innovation potential of blockchain technology. An example of this approach might be a CBDC that uses a private, permissioned blockchain for certain operations while relying on traditional databases for others.

- **Security Considerations:** Security is a paramount consideration in CBDC development. While blockchain offers enhanced security features like cryptographic protection and resistance to tampering, traditional databases provide more control over access and can implement robust security protocols aligned with existing financial security standards.

- **Scalability and Performance:** The scalability of blockchain technology, particularly in handling high volumes of transactions efficiently, remains a challenge for CBDCs. In contrast, traditional databases can manage large-scale transaction processing more effectively but might lack the distributed resilience and fault tolerance that blockchain offers.

- **Interoperability with Existing Systems:** The ability of a CBDC's technology to integrate seamlessly with existing financial systems is crucial for its adoption and effectiveness. Interoperability challenges range from technical integration to ensuring compliance with financial regulations, necessitating careful consideration in the choice of technology.

- **Innovation and Future Proofing:** The technological choice for CBDCs also impacts their capacity for future innovation. Blockchain technology, being relatively new and rapidly evolving, offers exciting prospects for future advancements in financial technology. In contrast, traditional databases, while more stable and tested, might offer fewer opportunities for innovative applications.

- **Interactive Element:** To engage readers further, consider posing questions like, "How do you think the choice of technology will impact the user experience of a CBDC?" or "What potential innovations could emerge from blockchain-based CBDCs?" These prompts encourage readers to think critically about the implications of technology choices in the development and use of CBDCs, fostering a deeper understanding of their potential impact on the financial landscape.

Objectives Behind Central Banks Adopting CBDCs

Central banks around the globe are on the brink of a revolutionary shift, embracing digital transformations that promise to redefine the financial landscape. But what drives this seismic shift? Let's embark on a journey to understand the multifaceted objectives fueling central banks' foray into the digital realm.

- **Improving Financial System Efficiency:** Central banks view CBDCs as a means to significantly enhance the efficiency of the financial system. By leveraging digital technologies, CBDCs promise to streamline payment processes, reducing the time and cost associated with transactions. This improvement is expected to be particularly impactful in cross-border payments, traditionally bogged down by multiple intermediaries and delays, thereby fostering smoother global trade.

- **Response to Decentralized Cryptocurrencies:** CBDCs also emerge as a strategic response to the burgeoning popularity of decentralized cryptocurrencies like Bitcoin. Central banks are increasingly concerned about the unregulated and often volatile nature of these digital assets. By introducing CBDCs, they aim to provide a safer, regulated alternative, hoping to preserve monetary sovereignty and mitigate the risks associated with unregulated digital currencies.

- **Enhancing Monetary Policy Tools:** CBDCs could revolutionize how central banks implement monetary policy. With digital currencies, central banks may gain more direct control over the money supply and have the ability to adjust interest rates more effectively. The concept of programmable money could also allow for more targeted economic interventions, such as direct stimulus payments to citizens.

- **Financial Inclusion Goals:** Promoting financial inclusion is another key objective behind CBDCs. In regions where traditional banking infrastructure is sparse, CBDCs offer a digital avenue to financial services, potentially bringing banking to millions of unbanked or underbanked individuals. This could significantly reduce financial disparities and stimulate economic growth in underprivileged areas.

- **Control as an Underlying Motive:** While the aforementioned benefits are often highlighted, it is critical to consider the underlying motive of control. CBDCs present an opportunity for central banks to regain some of the financial authority that might be eroded by decentralized cryptocurrencies, thus maintaining their pivotal role in the financial system.

- **Case Studies and Examples:** Countries like China with its digital yuan and the Bahamas with the Sand Dollar provide practical case studies.

These examples reveal how different nations are experimenting with CBDCs, each with distinct objectives like combating fraud, improving financial accessibility, or enhancing monetary policy efficiency.

- **Balancing Innovation and Control:** Central banks face the challenge of balancing the adoption of innovative technologies with the need to maintain control and stability in the financial system. This balancing act involves navigating complex issues such as privacy, security, and the potential disruption to existing banking structures.

- **Future Implications and Concerns:** The widespread adoption of CBDCs could have profound implications on financial independence and privacy. There are growing concerns around data security, surveillance potential, and the impact on traditional banks, which could see their roles diminish as digital currencies become more prevalent.

- **Interactive Element:** To engage the reader further, consider questions like, "Do you think CBDCs will effectively counter the rise of decentralized cryptocurrencies?" or "How might the implementation of CBDCs change the landscape of global finance?" These questions encourage readers to contemplate the broader impact of CBDCs on the financial ecosystem and their potential to shape future monetary policies and practices.

As we close this insightful section on the objectives behind CBDCs, we're left pondering their transformative potential. Will CBDCs redefine the very fabric of our financial interactions? Will they harmonize with or disrupt the existing monetary order? The answers lie ahead, in a future where tradition and innovation converge, crafting a new chapter in the story of money and finance.

Case Studies of CBDC Implementation

As we navigate the fascinating world of Central Bank Digital Currencies (CBDCs), let's delve into some intriguing case studies. These real-world examples offer a window into how different nations are embracing this digital financial revolution, each with its unique approach and set of challenges.

- **China's Digital Yuan (e-CNY) Initiative**: Begin with China's pioneering efforts in launching the Digital Yuan. Discuss the government's motivations, including enhancing domestic monetary policy and internationalizing the Yuan. Highlight the technology used, the pilot programs in various cities, and the public's response, especially in terms of privacy concerns and adoption rates.

- **The Bahamas' Sand Dollar**: Explore the Bahamas' Sand Dollar, one of the first fully deployed CBDCs. Focus on its objectives to boost financial inclusion in a region with many remote islands and enhance the resilience of the financial system against natural disasters. Discuss the technological infrastructure, the integration with local banks, and the impact on the local economy and population.

- **Sweden's E-Krona Project**: Delve into Sweden's E-Krona project, motivated by the country's move towards a cashless society. Examine the design choices, such as using a blockchain or not, the intended use cases, the concerns around digital literacy and accessibility, and the ongoing tests and evaluations.

- **Eastern Caribbean Central Bank's DCash**: Investigate the Eastern Caribbean Central Bank's DCash, a digital version of the Eastern Caribbean dollar. Highlight its aim to improve financial efficiency and integration among member states. Discuss the technology platform, user experience, and challenges faced in implementation.

- **The European Central Bank's Digital Euro Exploration**: Discuss the European Central Bank's exploration of a Digital Euro. Focus on its potential to strengthen the Eurozone's financial sovereignty, the considerations around privacy and security, and the implications for the broader European financial system.

- **India's Digital Rupee Trials**: Examine India's approach to testing a digital rupee. Discuss the government's objectives to enhance digital financial inclusion and combat corruption. Delve into the technology being considered, pilot programs, and potential impacts on India's vast and diverse financial landscape.

- **Canada's CBDC Contingency Planning**: Explore Canada's approach, focusing on contingency planning rather than immediate implementation. Discuss the rationale behind this approach, potential design features, and how it reflects the country's cautious stance on adopting a CBDC.

- **Interactive Element**: Include questions such as, "Which CBDC implementation strategy do you find most effective and why?" or "What lessons can be learned from these diverse approaches to CBDC implementation?"

- **Visual Aids**: Use infographics to compare and contrast the different CBDCs in terms of technology, adoption, and objectives.

- **Global Implications**: Conclude with a discussion on how these case studies reflect the diverse global perspectives on CBDCs and what they indicate about the future of digital currencies worldwide.

Reflecting on these stories, one wonders: how will the CBDCs evolve? Will they coexist with cryptocurrencies, or chart a different course? The answers lie in a future that's as exciting as it is unpredictable.

CBDCs' Impact on Traditional Banking and Finance

The advent of Central Bank Digital Currencies (CBDCs) heralds a transformation in the traditional banking and financial landscape. Let's unravel this intricate tapestry, examining the nuanced impacts CBDCs could have on the pillars of our established financial systems.

- **Redefining Banking Roles and Functions**: Start with an overview of how CBDCs could redefine the roles and functions of traditional banks. Discuss the possibility of banks evolving from being primary deposit holders to becoming service providers and intermediaries in a CBDC-dominated ecosystem.

- **Shift in Deposit and Lending Dynamics**: Delve into the potential shift in deposit and lending dynamics due to CBDCs. Explore how CBDCs might lead to a direct interaction between central banks and the public, potentially bypassing commercial banks, and what this means for the traditional deposit and loan system.

- **Impact on Financial Stability and Interest Rates**: Examine the potential implications of CBDCs on financial stability. Discuss scenarios where CBDCs could lead to increased central bank control over monetary policy, influencing interest rates, and liquidity in the economy.

- **Risk of Bank Disintermediation**: Investigate the risk of bank disintermediation posed by CBDCs. Discuss how the safety and accessibility of CBDCs might lead consumers to prefer them over bank deposits, potentially affecting the banks' ability to lend and create credit.

- **The Challenge of Balancing Innovation and Regulation**: Explore how banks and financial institutions are preparing to balance the innovative potential of CBDCs with the need for regulatory compliance. Discuss the evolving landscape of financial regulations in the wake of CBDCs.

- **Case Studies of Banks Adapting to CBDCs**: Present case studies of banks and financial institutions that are adapting to the emerging

CBDC landscape. Include examples of banks developing new financial products, services, or partnerships in response to CBDC initiatives.

- **Future of Financial Services with CBDCs**: Speculate on the future of financial services in a world where CBDCs are prevalent. Discuss how banks might innovate in providing digital financial services, customer relationship management, and new forms of financial advice in the age of CBDCs.

- **Interactive Element**: Include thought-provoking questions for the reader, like "How might your banking experience change with the introduction of CBDCs?" or "What new services would you expect from banks in a CBDC-led financial system?"

- **Visual Aids**: Use diagrams and flowcharts to illustrate the flow of money in a traditional banking system versus a CBDC-inclusive system, highlighting key differences and impacts.

- **Concluding Insights**: Wrap up with insights on the balance between maintaining traditional banking strengths and embracing the new opportunities and challenges brought by CBDCs. Encourage readers to reflect on the potential transformations in the banking sector.

In conclusion, the journey of CBDCs in the world of banking and finance is akin to navigating uncharted waters. It's a story of adaptation, innovation, and resilience. The future chapters of this story will be written by the choices of policymakers, the reaction of traditional financial institutions, and the embrace of the public. As we turn the pages, we eagerly anticipate how this narrative will unfold, shaping the future of money and finance.

Global Regulatory Landscape for CBDCs

In the realm of Central Bank Digital Currencies (CBDCs), the global regulatory landscape is as varied and colorful as a patchwork quilt. Each country, with its unique economic backdrop and monetary policies, approaches the regulation of CBDCs with a distinct set of priorities and concerns.

- **Diverse National Approaches:** Take a world tour of CBDC regulation, and you'll see a spectrum of strategies. For instance, in Sweden, where cash usage has dwindled, the Riksbank is exploring the e-krona to complement cash. Meanwhile, in the Bahamas, the Sand Dollar aims to enhance financial inclusion in its archipelagic state. Contrast these with China's digital yuan, where the focus is on internationalizing its currency and enhancing domestic monetary policy.

- **Challenges in Universal Frameworks:** Crafting a one-size-fits-all regulatory framework for CBDCs is akin to threading a needle in a hurricane. The complexity arises from differing national financial systems, levels of economic development, and varied legal structures. The question that looms large is: how can a universal framework accommodate such diverse national interests and economic conditions?

- **Potential for International Collaboration:** Imagine a scenario where nations collaborate on CBDCs like astronauts on an international space station. Such collaboration could pave the way for seamless cross-border transactions, reduce currency conversion costs, and even combat financial crimes more effectively. However, this requires navigating the choppy waters of international politics and economic rivalries.

- **Risk of Conflict and Competition:** Now, switch the lens to the darker side of this narrative – the potential for conflict. Countries might weaponize their digital currencies in economic warfare, or engage in competitive devaluations. The race to launch CBDCs could spark tensions, particularly if they start to challenge the dominance of traditional reserve currencies like the US dollar.

- **Balancing National Sovereignty and Global Interoperability:** It's a tightrope walk for nations to balance their monetary sovereignty with the need for global interoperability of CBDCs. The challenge is to retain control over national monetary policies while ensuring that CBDCs are compatible across borders. It's like trying to harmonize different musical instruments to play a symphony.

- **Regulatory Innovations and Experimentation:** Some countries are turning to regulatory sandboxes, allowing them to test and refine CBDCs in a controlled environment. This approach is like training wheels for CBDCs, helping to understand their impact on the financial system before a full-scale rollout.

- **Future of Global CBDC Regulations:** Looking into the crystal ball, the future of CBDC regulation could involve a blend of national policies and international agreements. Think of it as a digital Bretton Woods, establishing ground rules for the new age of digital currency.

- **Interactive Reflection:** Picture this – you're a global financial regulator in the era of CBDCs. What would be your top priority in regulating a digital currency? Would you focus on financial stability, international interoperability, or perhaps the protection of consumer privacy?

In wrapping up this kaleidoscope of the global regulatory landscape for CBDCs, it's clear that the journey is as complex as it is exciting. Navigating this terrain will require a mix of innovation, collaboration, and perhaps a sprinkle of regulatory magic.

Potential Future Scenarios with CBDC Dominance

Intro: Imagine a future where Central Bank Digital Currencies (CBDCs) are the new norm, a digital symphony orchestrating the global financial landscape. In this visionary chapter, we explore the horizon of possibilities and challenges in a world dominated by CBDCs. From transforming international trade to reshaping individual financial autonomy, let's dive into the kaleidoscope of potential futures that CBDCs might unveil.

- **Revolutionizing Global Finance:** In a CBDC-dominated world, global finance could undergo a metamorphosis. Transactions, swifter than ever, could occur in real-time across borders, drastically reducing the time and cost associated with international payments. Imagine a world where trade is not just a matter of hours but minutes, fostering a more interconnected global economy.

- **International Trade Transformation:** CBDCs could redefine international trade dynamics. With streamlined currency conversions and reduced transaction costs, small and medium-sized enterprises (SMEs) might find themselves on a more level playing field with larger corporations. The ease of cross-border transactions could open new markets, fostering a surge in global entrepreneurship and innovation.

- **Marginalization of Decentralized Cryptocurrencies:** A CBDC-dominated scenario could lead to the marginalization of decentralized cryptocurrencies. Central banks might assert their dominance through regulated digital currencies, offering stability and trust that decentralized cryptocurrencies struggle to match. However, in the shadow of CBDCs, cryptocurrencies might still thrive as niche assets or in regions where trust in central authorities is low.

- **Impacts on Financial Privacy and Autonomy:** The ascendancy of CBDCs raises profound questions about financial privacy and individual autonomy. With transactions potentially traceable and governments wielding greater oversight, the balance between security and privacy becomes a pivotal concern. Could this lead to a financial 'Big Brother,' or will privacy-preserving technologies emerge to protect individual rights?

- **Innovation in Financial Services:** The rise of CBDCs could spur innovation in financial services. Banks and fintech companies might develop new products and services tailored to a digital currency ecosystem, such as advanced financial management tools, personalized spending analytics, and integrated cross-platform services.

- **Challenges and Opportunities for the Unbanked:** CBDCs could present both challenges and opportunities for the unbanked population. On one hand, they offer a potential gateway to financial inclusion. On the other, there's a risk of exacerbating the digital divide if not implemented with considerations for access and education.

- **Regulatory Evolution:** The dominance of CBDCs would necessitate an evolution in regulatory frameworks, both nationally and internationally. This could lead to greater cooperation between countries in setting standards for digital currency usage, combating financial crimes, and ensuring a stable global financial system.

- **Interactive Element:** Engage the reader with questions like, "How do you envision your daily financial transactions in a world dominated by CBDCs?" or "What role do you see decentralized cryptocurrencies playing in a CBDC-centric financial landscape?"

As we close this section, we're left to ponder the vast and varied implications of a CBDC-dominated future. It's a world brimming with potential, marked by rapid innovation, and yet shadowed by concerns over privacy and autonomy. The journey towards this future is as complex as it is fascinating, a path that will undoubtedly be shaped by technological advancements, policy decisions, and the evolving needs of a global society. In this brave new world, the very essence of money as we know it might be transformed, heralding a new era in the story of global currency.

As we conclude Chapter 6, we have gained a deeper understanding of Central Bank Digital Currencies and their potential role in the future financial landscape. We've explored the complexities, opportunities, and challenges that CBDCs present, and how they contrast with decentralized digital currencies. Moving forward, the development and implementation of CBDCs will undoubtedly be a key area to watch, as they hold the potential to significantly influence both national and global economic structures.

Chapter 7
The Challenges of Centralization

Centralized Control and Monetary Sovereignty

As we venture into the realm of Central Bank Digital Currencies (CBDCs) and centralized digital currencies, a pivotal issue emerges - the balance of power between states and citizens, and the inherent risks of centralized control.

- **Centralization and Oversight:** At the heart of CBDCs lies a key characteristic: centralization. Unlike decentralized cryptocurrencies, CBDCs are tightly controlled by central authorities, typically the nation's central bank. This centralization grants governments unprecedented oversight over financial transactions. Every digital token can be traced, every transaction logged, and every financial movement monitored. This level of oversight has profound implications for individual privacy and financial autonomy.

- **The Double-Edged Sword of Monetary Sovereignty:** Centralized digital currencies reinforce the concept of monetary sovereignty. While this empowers states to exercise greater control over their economies, streamline monetary policies, and combat financial crimes more effectively, it also raises questions about the extent of government surveillance. The ability of a state to monitor and potentially regulate every financial transaction of its citizens might lead to concerns about an Orwellian financial system where Big Brother is always watching.

- **Systemic Risks in Infrastructure:** Centralized digital currencies, including CBDCs, are heavily reliant on robust technological infrastructure. This reliance is a vulnerability - a single point of failure in the system, be it a power outage, cyberattack, or an internet shutdown, could cripple the entire financial network. Unlike decentralized systems, where the distributed ledger provides resilience against such systemic risks, centralized systems are more susceptible to disruptions.

- **Examples and Case Studies:** Consider the case of a hypothetical country implementing a CBDC. If a major cyberattack were to occur, disrupting the central servers, it could freeze all digital financial transactions nationwide, leading to economic standstill. Or, in a scenario where internet access is restricted, individuals in remote areas might be unable to access their funds, exacerbating financial inequality.

- **Balancing Act:** Governments and central banks are thus faced with a balancing act. On one hand, they must harness the efficiency, control, and oversight that CBDCs offer. On the other, they must mitigate the risks of over-centralization, systemic vulnerabilities, and the potential erosion of financial privacy.

- **Future Perspectives:** Looking forward, the challenge lies in developing CBDC systems that maintain state sovereignty and economic stability while respecting individual privacy and autonomy. Innovations in technology might offer solutions - for example, advanced encryption techniques to protect user privacy or decentralized nodes within a centralized system to enhance resilience against systemic failures.

- **Interactive Element:** As readers, we must ponder – how much control should a government have over individual finances? What safeguards should be in place to protect financial privacy in a digital age dominated by CBDCs? These questions are not just theoretical but are at the forefront of shaping the future of money and finance.

In conclusion, the journey of centralized digital currencies, especially CBDCs, is laden with both opportunities and challenges. Navigating these waters requires a nuanced understanding of the delicate balance between efficiency, control, and individual rights. As this story unfolds, it is incumbent upon policymakers, technologists, and citizens to collaboratively chart a course that steers us toward a secure, efficient, and equitable financial future.

Privacy Concerns in Government-Managed Digital Currencies

In the evolving landscape of Central Bank Digital Currencies (CBDCs), privacy emerges as a pivotal concern. The integration of CBDCs into the financial fabric of society brings with it not just the promise of technological advancement but also the looming shadow of increased governmental oversight and control over personal financial transactions.

- **Inherent Privacy Risks with CBDCs:** The design of CBDCs inherently enables the tracking and monitoring of transactions. Every digital transaction made with a CBDC will be recorded, leaving a digital trail accessible to the central bank and the government. This feature raises significant concerns about the level of surveillance and monitoring governments will exercise over individual financial activities.

- **The 'Big Brother' Scenario:** The potential for a 'Big Brother' scenario is starkly evident. Governments, under the pretext of regulatory compliance, will have the capacity to scrutinize spending patterns extensively. There's a realistic possibility that purchases not aligning with a government's policies or ideologies will be flagged. This capability will give governments unprecedented power to influence or even control individual spending behaviors, effectively policing personal choices and lifestyles through financial means.

- **Case Studies of Concern:** Taking the example of China's digital yuan, the integration of this CBDC with existing digital payment platforms signifies the government's ability to access extensive transaction data. In other countries experimenting with CBDCs, there's a realistic worry about how transaction data will be used and potentially abused, especially in contexts of political dissent or suppression of minority groups.

- **Efficiency at the Expense of Privacy:** The pressing challenge for governments and central banks is managing the trade-off between the control offered by CBDCs and the privacy rights of citizens. While technological innovations might propose solutions for anonymity, the overarching trend suggests that governments will prioritize control and oversight over privacy concerns.

- **Regulatory and Oversight Dilemmas:** The introduction of CBDCs will necessitate stringent legal frameworks and oversight mechanisms, yet there's a genuine risk that these regulations will serve more to consolidate governmental control rather than protect privacy. Transparent policies on data usage may be promised, but the reality could be a landscape where data collection becomes a tool for monitoring and controlling citizen behavior.

- **Future Implications for Civil Liberties:** The future implications of CBDCs on civil liberties are profound and somewhat alarming. While they represent a significant leap in financial technology, they also pose a grave risk to the right to privacy. The potential for governments to limit or block purchases that don't align with their policies or beliefs is a realistic concern, turning CBDCs into instruments of financial censorship.

Reflecting on these scenarios, it becomes clear that the narrative of CBDCs is not just about financial innovation but also about the balance of power between the state and the individual. Questions arise: To what extent will our financial autonomy be compromised? How will the convenience of digital currencies reshape our fundamental freedoms? These are not hypothetical questions but real concerns that will define the future of money and our place within its narrative.

Data Security and Vulnerability in Centralized Digital Currencies

The shift towards centralized digital currencies, such as CBDCs, brings to the fore critical issues of data security and vulnerability. In a digital age where financial transactions are increasingly moving online, the risks associated with cyberattacks, data breaches, and system failures become more pronounced, particularly in systems centralized under government or financial institution control.

- **Cybersecurity Threats:** Centralized digital currencies are prime targets for cybercriminals. The consolidation of financial data in a single system creates a 'honeypot' effect, where the potential payoff for successful hacks is immense. Cyberattacks could range from theft of financial assets to compromising the integrity of financial data. The implications of such attacks are not just financial but also socio-economic, as they could erode public trust in digital financial systems.

- **Data Breaches and Financial Privacy:** Data breaches in a centralized digital currency system could lead to massive leaks of personal and financial information. In an era where data is as valuable as currency itself, the exposure of personal transaction histories could lead to identity theft, financial fraud, and a significant invasion of privacy. These breaches can have long-lasting effects on individuals' lives, far beyond the immediate financial losses.

- **System Failures and Dependence:** The reliance on centralized systems for financial transactions introduces the risk of system failures. Unlike decentralized systems where the failure of one node doesn't incapacitate the network, centralized systems are vulnerable to single points of failure. These could arise from technical faults, power outages, or even natural disasters, leading to widespread disruption in financial services and potential economic chaos.

- **The Challenge of Securing a Centralized System:** Securing a centralized digital currency system is a complex and ongoing challenge. It involves not only robust encryption and cybersecurity measures but also continuous monitoring and updating of security protocols. The dynamic nature of cyber threats means that systems must evolve constantly to stay ahead of hackers.

- **Potential Catastrophic Consequences:** The consequences of a major security breach or system failure in a centralized digital currency system could be catastrophic. They could lead to a loss of billions in financial assets, erode public confidence in digital currencies, and even destabilize national economies. The recovery from such an event could take years and would require significant resources.

- **International Implications:** In an interconnected global economy, the security vulnerabilities of one nation's centralized digital currency system could have international repercussions. A breach in one system could lead to ripple effects through global financial markets, affecting international trade and economic relations.

- **Moving Forward with Caution:** As central banks and governments explore the realm of digital currencies, they must proceed with caution, prioritizing data security and system resilience. This involves not only leveraging advanced technology but also fostering international cooperation in cybersecurity and establishing rigorous regulatory standards.

As we delve into this digital future, questions arise about the balance between innovation and security. How do we protect such centralized systems from evolving cyber threats? What contingency plans are necessary to mitigate the impacts of system failures? These questions underscore the need for a cautious and thoughtful approach to the development and implementation of centralized digital currencies.

Exclusionary Risks of CBDCs

The implementation of Central Bank Digital Currencies (CBDCs) heralds a significant shift in the financial landscape, potentially reshaping access to economic resources. However, this shift isn't without its challenges, particularly in terms of financial inclusion. CBDCs, while designed to streamline financial operations, could inadvertently create barriers for certain segments of society.

- **Technology Access:** The very foundation of CBDCs – their digital nature – can be a significant hurdle. For individuals in regions with limited or unreliable internet access, or for those who cannot afford smartphones or computers, CBDCs may be practically inaccessible. This digital divide could exacerbate existing inequalities in financial access, leaving behind those who are already marginalized in the banking system.

- **Digital Literacy:** The effective use of CBDCs requires a degree of digital literacy that not all individuals possess. The elderly, people in rural areas, and those with limited education may find navigating digital currency platforms challenging. Without proper education and resources to improve digital literacy, these populations could find themselves excluded from the benefits of CBDCs.

- **Marginalization of Vulnerable Groups:** Certain groups who already face challenges in accessing traditional banking services, such as low-income families, migrants, or people without stable housing, may find these challenges magnified in a digital economy. The requirement for identification and digital registration for using CBDCs could be an insurmountable barrier for people in these situations.

- **Potential for Systemic Bias:** The algorithms and systems underpinning CBDCs could inadvertently perpetuate systemic biases. If these digital platforms are not designed with inclusivity in mind, they could reinforce existing financial inequalities, rather than alleviate them.

This scenario necessitates a conscious effort to embed fairness and accessibility in the design of CBDC systems.

- **Bridging the Digital Divide:** For CBDCs to be truly inclusive, concerted efforts must be made to bridge the digital divide. This includes investing in infrastructure to ensure widespread internet access, providing affordable digital devices, and delivering comprehensive digital education programs.

- **Tailoring Solutions for Inclusivity:** Designing CBDC platforms with inclusivity at their core is crucial. This means creating user-friendly interfaces that are accessible to people with varying levels of education and digital proficiency. Additionally, providing offline solutions or hybrid models could ensure that those without constant internet access are not left out.

- **Legal and Policy Frameworks:** Legal and policy frameworks need to be established to protect the rights of all individuals in the digital economy. This includes ensuring privacy, preventing discrimination, and setting up safeguards against digital fraud and scams that might disproportionately affect vulnerable populations.

As we venture into this new era of digital currencies, it's vital to reflect on the broader societal implications. Questions arise, such as: How can we ensure CBDCs are accessible to everyone, regardless of their socioeconomic status or digital prowess? What measures can be taken to prevent financial exclusion in the digital age? The answers to these questions will shape the degree to which CBDCs can offer a more inclusive financial future.

Impact on the Traditional Banking Sector

The introduction of Central Bank Digital Currencies (CBDCs) is poised to disrupt the traditional banking sector significantly, altering its landscape in profound ways. This imminent change raises several questions about the future role of commercial banks, their profitability, and the very structure of the banking industry.

- **Transformation of Commercial Banks' Roles:** With the advent of CBDCs, commercial banks could see a dramatic shift in their conventional roles. Traditionally, these institutions have acted as intermediaries in financial transactions, providing services like loans, deposits, and payment processing. However, CBDCs could enable direct transactions between consumers and the central bank, bypassing commercial banks entirely. This shift would require banks to redefine their roles, possibly focusing more on advisory services, investment management, and other non-transaction-based services.

- **Reduced Profitability and Revenue Streams:** One of the most significant impacts of CBDCs on traditional banks would be on their profitability. Banks currently earn substantial revenues from transaction fees, account management fees, and interest margins. With CBDCs potentially offering cheaper and more efficient transaction methods, banks might lose a significant portion of this revenue. They would need to explore new revenue models or enhance existing ones, such as wealth management or specialized financial products tailored to specific customer needs.

- **Risk of Disintermediation:** The direct relationship that CBDCs foster between central banks and the public poses a disintermediation risk for traditional banks. If individuals and businesses can deposit their funds directly with the central bank, the role of commercial banks as deposit-takers could diminish. This shift could lead to a significant restructuring of the banking industry, with banks needing to diversify their services and offerings to remain relevant.

- **Adapting to Technological Change:** To remain competitive in a CBDC-driven financial landscape, traditional banks would need to embrace technological innovation. This might include integrating CBDC transactions into their existing digital platforms, adopting blockchain technology for improved security and efficiency, and exploring new fintech partnerships to enhance their service offerings.

- **Impact on Lending Practices:** The traditional model of banks taking deposits and using them to lend may be challenged by CBDCs. Banks would need to innovate their lending practices, potentially relying more on alternative funding sources. They might also need to focus on more value-added services in lending, such as personalized lending solutions or sector-specific financing.

- **Regulatory Adaptations:** As CBDCs redefine the banking landscape, regulatory frameworks would need to evolve. Banks would need to navigate these changes, ensuring compliance while also advocating for regulations that support a level playing field and foster healthy competition between traditional banks and new digital currency systems.

- **Building Trust and Customer Relationships:** In a CBDC-dominated world, maintaining customer trust and relationships would become more crucial than ever for banks. They would need to leverage their established reputations and customer service excellence to retain and attract customers, emphasizing the human element and personalized advice that digital currencies cannot provide.

- **Future Banking Models:** Looking ahead, it's clear that the banking sector must prepare for transformative changes. Banks might evolve into entities that focus more on specialized financial services, advisory roles, and financial technology innovation. They would need to be agile, adapting to the changing financial landscape while finding new ways to add value to their customers' financial lives.

The journey of traditional banks in the era of CBDCs will be one of adaptation, innovation, and perhaps, reinvention. As these institutions navigate this new terrain, their ability to respond to these changes will determine their place in the future of finance.

Economic Surveillance and Individual Autonomy

The rise of Central Bank Digital Currencies (CBDCs) brings with it a potent capability for economic surveillance that raises critical questions about individual financial autonomy and freedom. This new landscape of digital finance offers unprecedented access to transaction data, presenting a double-edged sword in terms of privacy and control.

- **Unprecedented Access to Financial Data:** CBDCs provide governments with direct access to vast amounts of financial transaction data. Every digital transaction made using a CBDC could potentially be traced, tracked, and analyzed. This capability extends far beyond what is possible with traditional cash transactions, giving governments a granular view of economic activity at both the individual and collective levels.

- **Implications for Financial Privacy:** The potential for CBDCs to be used as tools for economic surveillance raises significant privacy concerns. In a world where financial transactions are completely digitized and traceable, the privacy of individuals' spending habits could be severely compromised. The ability of a government to monitor and analyze every transaction poses a risk to the fundamental right to financial privacy.

- **Control over Spending:** Beyond privacy concerns, there's the possibility of governments exerting control over individual spending through CBDCs. In extreme scenarios, governments could use this technology to block transactions for certain goods or services, or even restrict transactions with certain entities. This level of control would represent a significant shift in the balance of power between states and citizens, fundamentally altering the concept of financial freedom.

- **Impact on Financial Autonomy:** The transition to CBDCs could also impact individual financial autonomy. With traditional cash, individuals have a degree of anonymity and independence in their transactions. However, CBDCs could enable governments to impose restrictions or conditions on the use of money, potentially leading to scenarios where financial autonomy is curtailed.

- **Ethical and Societal Implications:** The ethical implications of such surveillance are profound. They bring into question issues of trust, the role of the state in private transactions, and the ethical use of financial data. Societal implications are equally significant, with potential impacts on consumer behavior, economic freedom, and the relationship between citizens and the state.

- **Balancing Surveillance with Privacy:** One of the greatest challenges in the deployment of CBDCs will be finding a balance between the benefits of economic surveillance (such as preventing financial crimes) and the protection of individual privacy and autonomy. This will require careful design of CBDC systems, robust legal frameworks, and perhaps most importantly, transparent and accountable governance.

- **International Perspectives:** Different countries may approach this balance in various ways, reflecting their cultural, political, and social norms. In some jurisdictions, privacy may be prioritized, while in others, the emphasis might be on the benefits of surveillance for state security and economic policy.

- **Future of Financial Freedom:** Looking ahead, the conversation around CBDCs and economic surveillance will continue to evolve. It will shape not just the future of finance but also broader debates about privacy, autonomy, and the role of technology in society.

As we stand at the crossroads of a digital financial revolution, it is crucial to engage in open and thoughtful discourse about these issues. The decisions made today will define the landscape of money and freedom for generations to come.

Global Financial Stability and CBDCs

The introduction of Central Bank Digital Currencies (CBDCs) stands to significantly reshape the global financial landscape. As nations contemplate or advance towards adopting CBDCs, it's crucial to consider their potential impact on global financial stability. This new frontier of digital currency brings with it both opportunities and challenges that could reverberate across the world's economic systems.

- **Potential for Rapid Currency Devaluations:** One of the critical concerns with CBDCs is their susceptibility to rapid devaluations. Unlike physical currencies, digital currencies can be more volatile due to the speed at which digital transactions occur. In scenarios where there's a loss of confidence in a particular CBDC, this could lead to a swift devaluation, affecting not just the domestic economy but also international trade partners. Such volatility could pose significant risks to global financial stability, especially if large economies experience fluctuations in their digital currency value.

- **Impact on International Trade:** CBDCs have the potential to streamline international trade by reducing transaction times and costs. However, they also raise concerns about exchange rate stability and monetary policy transmission. If each country operates its digital currency, this could lead to complex dynamics in trade relationships. For instance, countries might engage in competitive devaluations of their digital currencies to boost exports, leading to trade imbalances and tension.

- **Economic Contagion in a Digital World:** In a world where CBDCs are dominant, economic contagion – the spread of economic crises or shocks from one country to others – could become more pronounced. Given the interconnected nature of digital currencies and the rapidity of digital transactions, a financial crisis in one nation could swiftly impact others. This interconnectedness demands robust international regulatory frameworks and coordination to safeguard against such contagion.

- **Managing Cross-Border Flows:** The ease of cross-border transactions with CBDCs could lead to more significant capital flows, both in and out of countries. While this can boost investment and economic growth, it also poses risks of capital flight, especially in times of economic instability. Managing these flows will be a critical challenge for maintaining global financial stability.

- **Harmonization of Regulatory Frameworks:** A key aspect in ensuring financial stability with the advent of CBDCs is the harmonization of international regulatory frameworks. Different regulatory standards across countries could lead to regulatory arbitrage, where entities exploit these differences to bypass stricter regulations. Developing cohesive and comprehensive global regulatory standards for CBDCs will be crucial in maintaining financial stability.

- **Technological Risks and Systemic Failures:** The reliance on technology in a CBDC-driven financial system introduces risks of systemic failures due to technical glitches, cyberattacks, or infrastructure breakdowns. Such incidents could have far-reaching implications, quickly transmitting shocks across global financial systems.

- **Addressing Inequalities in Global Finance:** CBDCs also present an opportunity to address existing inequalities in global finance, such as unequal access to banking services and credit. However, if not managed inclusively, CBDCs could exacerbate these inequalities, particularly if advanced economies move ahead rapidly leaving others behind.

- **Preparing for the Future:** In preparing for a world where CBDCs play a central role, policymakers, financial institutions, and international bodies must collaborate to address these challenges. This includes developing strategies to manage the risks of currency devaluations, economic contagion, and regulatory disparities.

In conclusion, the journey towards a CBDC-dominated financial world is fraught with complexities that require careful navigation. The potential for enhancing global financial stability is significant, but so are the risks. As the narrative of CBDCs unfolds, it will be a test of international cooperation and foresight in shaping a stable and equitable digital financial future.

Chapter 8
CBDCs and the Future of Traditional Banking

Transformation of Banking Business Models

The introduction of Central Bank Digital Currencies (CBDCs) marks a watershed moment in the history of banking, poised to transform traditional banking business models fundamentally. This evolution will challenge the very essence of how banks have operated for centuries.

- **Revolution in Deposit and Lending:** The quintessential functions of commercial banks – accepting deposits and extending loans – face a seismic shift with the advent of CBDCs. When a central bank issues digital currency directly to the public, it assumes roles traditionally reserved for commercial banks. This transition could lead to a decline in deposits with commercial banks as individuals and businesses might prefer holding their funds in CBDCs, perceived as more secure being backed by the central bank. As deposits dwindle, banks' ability to create loans could be significantly impacted, necessitating a profound rethinking of their role in the financial ecosystem.

- **Service-Based Banking Model:** In this new landscape, banks might pivot towards service-oriented models. Here, instead of relying on interest from deposits and loans for revenue, banks could focus on providing value-added services. These could include financial advisory, wealth management, and bespoke financial products tailored to individual needs. Banks might also evolve to become intermediaries in handling CBDC transactions, ensuring compliance, providing cybersecurity, and offering customer support.

- **Impact on Interest Rates and Revenue Streams:** With CBDCs, central banks might directly influence interest rates for end-users, bypassing traditional banking channels. This direct control could compress banks' interest margins, pushing them to innovate alternative revenue streams beyond interest-based income.

- **Technology and Innovation as Key Drivers:** Banks would need to invest heavily in technology to stay relevant. This involves not just adopting but also innovating in digital platforms, cybersecurity measures, and customer interface systems. As CBDCs operate on advanced digital frameworks, banks' technological prowess will be a significant competitive differentiator.

- **Potential for New Partnerships:** CBDCs could encourage new forms of partnerships between commercial banks and fintech companies. Banks might leverage fintech innovations to enhance their service offerings, manage digital transactions more efficiently, and provide enriched customer experiences.

- **Challenges in Transition:** This transformation won't be without challenges. Banks will need to navigate a landscape where their traditional roles are diminishing while simultaneously building new capabilities in uncharted territories. Regulatory compliance, cybersecurity, and managing digital identity will be crucial areas requiring attention.

- **Redefining Customer Relationships:** The relationship between banks and their customers will undergo a transformation. In a CBDC-dominated world, banks will need to offer more than just financial transactions; they will need to build relationships based on trust, advisory, and personalized services.

- **The Future of Banking Employees:** The shift in business models will also have implications for banking professionals. Skills in digital technologies, customer relationship management, and advisory services will be in higher demand, transforming the nature of banking jobs.

In conclusion, CBDCs represent not just a technological advancement but a catalyst for a paradigm shift in banking. While they pose significant challenges to the traditional banking model, they also offer opportunities for banks to reinvent themselves, focusing more on customer service and innovative solutions. Banks that can successfully navigate this transformation will emerge stronger, more agile, and more attuned to the needs of the digital age.

Disintermediation and Its Consequences

The rise of Central Bank Digital Currencies (CBDCs) brings to the fore the concept of disintermediation, a pivotal change where individuals and businesses might prefer transacting directly with central banks, bypassing traditional commercial banks. This shift could lead to significant repercussions for the banking sector and the broader financial landscape.

- **Bypassing Traditional Banks:** The direct relationship between central banks and the public through CBDCs could lead to a significant reduction in the role of commercial banks as intermediaries. Customers, attracted by the security and efficiency of CBDCs, may choose to keep their funds with central banks, reducing their reliance on commercial banks. This fundamental shift would disrupt the traditional deposit-taking model that banks have long relied on.

- **Impact on Deposits and Liquidity:** One of the immediate consequences of disintermediation is the potential loss of deposits for commercial banks. Deposits are a primary source of capital for banks, used to create loans and generate interest income. With the outflow of deposits to central banks, the liquidity available to commercial banks could drastically reduce, limiting their ability to lend and potentially leading to higher interest rates to attract depositors.

- **Shrinking of the Banking Sector:** As CBDCs gain traction, there could be a corresponding shrinkage in the banking sector. Banks may find it challenging to maintain their current scale of operations in the face of reduced deposits and loan capabilities. This could lead to consolidation in the industry, with smaller banks either merging with larger entities or exiting the market altogether.

- **Reduced Profit Margins:** The profitability of banks is also likely to be affected. With a smaller base of deposits and a reduced lending capacity, banks' profit margins could shrink. They would need to seek alternative revenue streams, potentially shifting towards non-interest income sources such as fees for financial services and advisory.

- **Innovation as a Response:** To counter the effects of disintermediation, banks will need to innovate and diversify their services. This could include offering more sophisticated digital banking solutions, personalized financial products, and investing in technology to improve customer experience and operational efficiency.

- **Role of Banks in a CBDC World:** Banks may need to redefine their roles in a financial ecosystem with CBDCs. They could become facilitators and integrators of CBDC transactions, offering value-added services around the digital currency ecosystem. Their role could shift towards advisory, risk management, and financial planning services for both individuals and businesses.

- **Challenges in Transition:** Banks will face significant challenges in transitioning to this new environment. Adapting to the reduced role in deposits and payments, re-skilling employees, and upgrading technological infrastructure would require substantial investment and strategic planning.

- **Opportunities for Collaboration:** There could be opportunities for banks to collaborate with central banks in the CBDC ecosystem. They might act as intermediaries in distributing CBDCs or provide complementary services that central banks may not offer, such as complex financial products, wealth management, or cross-border financial services.

In conclusion, the advent of CBDCs and the resulting disintermediation represent both a challenge and an opportunity for the traditional banking sector. Banks that successfully navigate this new landscape by innovating, diversifying, and collaborating will likely emerge resilient and relevant in the age of digital currencies. The future of banking, in the era of CBDCs, will be marked by adaptability, technological advancement, and a keen focus on customer-centric services.

Interest Rates and Monetary Policy

The advent of Central Bank Digital Currencies (CBDCs) could substantially reshape the landscape of monetary policy and interest rate management. These digital currencies, controlled directly by central banks, present both opportunities and challenges in the realms of economic governance.

- **Direct Control for Precision in Policy Implementation:** One of the most significant changes CBDCs bring to monetary policy is the unprecedented level of control and precision they offer central banks. With CBDCs, central banks can implement policy changes more efficiently and effectively. For instance, changes in interest rates could be enacted swiftly and uniformly across the economy, impacting all holders of the digital currency instantly. This direct control could lead to more responsive and targeted policy measures, allowing central banks to react more quickly to economic fluctuations.

- **Impact on Interest Rates:** The ease of implementing policy changes with CBDCs could lead to a more dynamic interest rate environment. Central banks might adjust rates more frequently to address economic conditions, potentially leading to greater fluctuations in borrowing costs for consumers and businesses. On the other hand, the precision of CBDCs could also allow for more subtle and nuanced interest rate policies, avoiding broad strokes that might otherwise impact the economy unevenly.

- **Challenges in Balancing Economic Objectives:** Despite these advantages, the use of CBDCs in monetary policy also presents significant challenges. Central banks will need to carefully balance objectives like economic growth and inflation control in an environment where their policy tools could have more direct and immediate impacts. The risk of over-correcting or underestimating the effects of policy changes becomes more pronounced with the powerful lever that CBDCs represent.

- **Potential for Programmable Money:** One fascinating aspect of CBDCs in monetary policy is the concept of programmable money. This would allow central banks to implement policies that could, for example, encourage spending in specific sectors or discourage it in others, based on pre-set rules encoded into the currency itself. While this could significantly enhance policy effectiveness, it also raises complex questions about economic freedom and the role of government in individual spending decisions.

- **Implications for Traditional Interest Rate Transmission:** The introduction of CBDCs might also alter the traditional mechanisms of interest rate transmission. With a more direct route to influence the economy, central banks might rely less on traditional tools like open market operations. This could lead to a fundamental shift in how monetary policy is conducted, with implications for financial markets, banking institutions, and the broader economy.

- **Risk of Rapid Capital Movements:** The ease of transferring CBDCs could lead to more rapid capital movements in response to interest rate changes. This could exacerbate economic volatility, especially in times of uncertainty, as individuals and businesses quickly adjust their holdings in response to policy shifts.

- **Global Implications:** On the international stage, the impact of CBDCs on monetary policy could lead to more pronounced global financial cycles. As major economies implement CBDCs, their monetary policy decisions could have more immediate and significant effects on global capital flows and exchange rates.

In summary, the integration of CBDCs into monetary policy frameworks presents a transformative shift. It offers central banks a powerful tool to fine-tune economic management but also requires a delicate balance to avoid unintended consequences. The future of monetary policy in the age of digital currencies will likely be characterized by innovation, adaptability, and an ongoing debate about the best ways to harness these new tools for economic stability and growth.

Financial Inclusion vs. Exclusion Paradox

Central Bank Digital Currencies (CBDCs) stand at the crossroads of financial inclusion and exclusion. While they promise to open up the financial system to the unbanked and underbanked, they also risk widening the digital divide.

- **Inclusive Potential of CBDCs:** At their core, CBDCs possess a transformative potential for financial inclusion. By digitizing currency, they can bring financial services to the fingertips of those who've been traditionally excluded due to a lack of physical banking infrastructure. In rural or remote areas where brick-and-mortar banks are scarce, CBDCs offer a lifeline, providing access to essential financial services like savings, transfers, and payments through a digital platform.

- **The Digital Divide Challenge:** However, this promising scenario hinges on a critical factor – digital accessibility. The efficacy of CBDCs in promoting financial inclusion is severely limited in regions with low internet penetration, lack of digital devices, or where populations lack the digital literacy to navigate these new financial tools. This gap creates a paradox where the very technology meant to include the excluded could inadvertently widen existing disparities.

- **Addressing the Digital Divide:** Tackling this challenge requires concerted efforts on multiple fronts. Governments and financial authorities need to invest in digital infrastructure, ensuring that internet and mobile network access reaches the farthest corners of their countries. Alongside infrastructure, there's a pressing need for digital education initiatives. These programs should be tailored to diverse populations, focusing on the basics of digital finance and the safe use of CBDCs.

- **Innovative Solutions for Accessibility:** Fintech innovation can play a crucial role in bridging the digital divide. For instance, the development of low-tech solutions for CBDC transactions, such as USSD-based mobile banking that doesn't require internet access, can be a game-changer. Similarly, public-private partnerships could facilitate the widespread distribution of affordable digital devices, making digital finance a reality for the masses.

- **Potential for Partially Offline CBDCs:** Another intriguing solution is the development of CBDC systems that can operate partially offline. By allowing limited transactions in offline modes, these systems could cater to populations in areas with unreliable internet connectivity, ensuring that financial inclusion isn't hamstrung by technological limitations.

- **User-Friendly Design:** Beyond technology, the design of CBDC platforms must prioritize user-friendliness. Intuitive interfaces and straightforward transaction processes can lower the barrier to entry, especially for populations new to digital finance.

- **Balancing Innovation with Inclusivity:** The journey of CBDCs towards financial inclusion must balance technological innovation with inclusivity. This means prioritizing the needs of the marginalized and structuring CBDC systems to be as accessible as possible.

- **Challenges and Opportunities:** The paradox of financial inclusion versus exclusion in the context of CBDCs presents both challenges and opportunities. It calls for innovative thinking, collaboration between various stakeholders, and a commitment to ensuring that the digital leap doesn't leave anyone behind.

In conclusion, while CBDCs hold immense potential for transforming the financial landscape, realizing this potential in an inclusive manner is a complex task. It requires addressing the digital divide head-on, through infrastructure development, educational initiatives, and technological innovations, ensuring that the shift to digital currency is equitable and inclusive for all.

Cybersecurity Threats in a CBDC-Dominated World

In a world where Central Bank Digital Currencies (CBDCs) play a pivotal role, cybersecurity emerges as a critical concern. The shift towards a CBDC-dominated financial landscape presents unique and complex cybersecurity challenges that must be meticulously addressed to protect the integrity of the financial system.

- **Systemic Risks in Digital Finance:** The adoption of CBDCs introduces systemic risks, particularly due to the centralized nature of these currencies. A successful cyberattack on a central bank's digital infrastructure could have far-reaching consequences, potentially destabilizing the entire financial system. Unlike decentralized cryptocurrencies, where risks are more distributed, the centralization of CBDCs means that a single point of failure could have catastrophic impacts.

- **The Digital Fortress:** Central banks, therefore, face the daunting task of building a digital fortress. This involves implementing state-of-the-art cybersecurity measures to protect against a spectrum of threats, from sophisticated hacking attempts to insider threats. Cybersecurity in a CBDC context goes beyond mere data protection; it encompasses safeguarding the currency's integrity, availability, and the trust of its users.

- **Challenges in Safeguarding Digital Currencies:** Safeguarding a digital currency system is a complex endeavor. It involves securing not just the currency's transaction and issuance processes but also ensuring the safety of users' data. This includes protection against hacking, phishing attacks, and other forms of cyber fraud. The complexity is heightened by the need to balance security with ease of use – making the system impenetrable to attackers while still user-friendly for the general public.

- **Potential Attack Scenarios:** Consider the myriad of cyberattack scenarios that could plague a CBDC system. These could range from distributed denial-of-service (DDoS) attacks, aiming to disrupt the currency's availability, to sophisticated attacks seeking to manipulate currency value or steal user funds. The interconnectivity of a CBDC system with other national and international financial networks further amplifies these risks.

- **The Implications of a Breach:** A breach in a central bank's digital currency system could lead to severe consequences. Apart from the immediate financial losses, such an incident could erode public trust in digital currencies, hampering their adoption and usage. In severe cases, it could lead to a financial crisis, especially if the breach undermines the currency's stability or leads to significant monetary theft.

- **Developing Robust Cybersecurity Frameworks:** Addressing these risks requires the development of robust cybersecurity frameworks, tailored specifically for CBDCs. This includes advanced encryption techniques, continuous monitoring systems, and regular stress testing of the CBDC infrastructure against potential cyber threats. Collaboration with cybersecurity experts, fintech innovators, and international bodies will be key in developing these comprehensive security measures.

- **Continuous Vigilance and Adaptation:** Cybersecurity in a CBDC-dominated world is not a one-time effort but a continuous process. As cyber threats evolve, so must the security measures guarding CBDCs. This involves not only technological upgrades but also adapting to changing cyber tactics and ensuring that cybersecurity protocols are always a step ahead of potential attackers.

- **The Role of Public Awareness:** Besides technological solutions, public awareness and education play a crucial role in cybersecurity. Educating CBDC users about safe digital practices, recognizing phishing attempts, and safeguarding their digital wallets can significantly reduce the risk of cyberattacks.

In conclusion, while CBDCs promise a revolutionary shift in the financial landscape, they bring with them an array of cybersecurity challenges. Navigating these challenges requires a multifaceted approach, combining advanced technology, continuous vigilance, and public awareness. The success of CBDCs will depend not just on their economic merits but also on the strength of their digital fortresses against the ever-evolving landscape of cyber threats.

Impact on Cross-Border Transactions and Forex Markets

The advent of Central Bank Digital Currencies (CBDCs) is poised to dramatically reshape the landscape of cross-border transactions and the foreign exchange (Forex) markets. This shift could herald a new era of international financial interactions, defined by unprecedented efficiency and accessibility.

- **Revolutionizing Cross-Border Transactions:** CBDCs promise to simplify the traditionally complex and costly process of cross-border transactions. Currently, these transactions often involve multiple intermediaries, each adding layers of fees and time delays. CBDCs, with their digital and centralized nature, could streamline this process, enabling direct and instantaneous transfers between countries. This transformation could significantly reduce transaction costs and processing times, making international trade and remittances more efficient.

- **Direct Impact on Forex Markets:** The introduction of CBDCs could have profound implications for Forex markets. Currently, currency exchange involves a complex web of banks and financial institutions, each taking a cut and adding to the overall cost of conversion. CBDCs could simplify this process, allowing for more direct and cost-effective currency conversions. This could lead to reduced transaction costs for businesses and individuals alike, potentially boosting international trade.

- **Potential Reduction in Currency Volatility:** One of the potential benefits of CBDCs in the context of Forex markets is the reduction of currency volatility. With more direct and efficient conversion mechanisms, CBDCs could lead to more stable exchange rates. This stability would be a boon for international businesses and investors, who currently have to navigate the uncertainties of fluctuating currencies.

- **Influence on International Trade Dynamics:** The efficiency and cost-effectiveness of CBDCs could influence international trade dynamics. By reducing the costs and complexities of cross-border transactions, CBDCs could make it easier for businesses to engage in international trade, potentially opening up new markets and opportunities, especially for smaller businesses that were previously hindered by high transaction costs.

- **Challenges and Considerations:** However, the integration of CBDCs into international transactions is not without its challenges. Issues such as interoperability between different CBDC systems, compliance with international regulations, and the impact on traditional banking institutions need to be carefully navigated. Additionally, there are concerns about the impact of this shift on countries with less developed digital infrastructures, and the potential for increased economic disparities.

- **Looking to the Future:** As we look to the future, the potential for CBDCs to transform cross-border transactions and Forex markets is immense. The prospect of more efficient, cost-effective, and stable international financial transactions could foster a more interconnected and prosperous global economy. However, the journey towards this future will require careful planning, international cooperation, and a commitment to ensuring that the benefits of this digital financial revolution are accessible to all.

In conclusion, CBDCs hold the promise of reshaping the very foundations of cross-border transactions and Forex markets. By offering a more streamlined, cost-effective, and stable means of conducting international financial transactions, they could significantly impact global trade and economic dynamics. However, realizing this potential will require overcoming significant challenges and ensuring that the transition to this new digital financial era is inclusive and equitable.

Adaptation Strategies for Traditional Banks

In a financial landscape increasingly dominated by Central Bank Digital Currencies (CBDCs), traditional banks face the critical challenge of adapting to remain relevant and competitive. This adaptation is not just a matter of survival but an opportunity to redefine their roles and services in a rapidly evolving digital economy.

- **New Service Offerings:** The emergence of CBDCs requires banks to rethink their service offerings. In a world where basic banking services like deposits and transactions can be directly managed by central banks, traditional banks might need to focus on providing more specialized and value-added services. These could include personalized financial advisory, wealth management, and bespoke investment solutions tailored to individual client needs. By leveraging their expertise and customer relationships, banks can offer a level of service and personalization that CBDC platforms may not be able to match.

- **Partnership Opportunities with Fintech Companies:** Collaboration with fintech companies presents a significant opportunity for traditional banks in the era of CBDCs. Fintech firms often lead in innovation, user experience, and digital agility – areas where traditional banks may lag. By forming strategic partnerships, banks can integrate cutting-edge technologies such as artificial intelligence, machine learning, and advanced analytics into their services. These technologies can enhance customer experience, streamline operations, and provide sophisticated tools for financial analysis and decision-making.

- **Adoption of Blockchain and Other Technologies:** To stay competitive, banks need to embrace the technologies underpinning CBDCs, notably blockchain. By adopting blockchain technology, banks can improve the efficiency, transparency, and security of their operations. Blockchain can be used to streamline processes such as KYC (Know Your Customer) compliance, fraud detection, and cross-border transactions. Moreover, blockchain can enable banks to offer innovative products like tokenized assets and smart contracts, aligning their services with the evolving digital economy.

- **Developing Digital Currency Solutions:** Banks should consider developing their digital currency solutions, compatible with CBDCs, to facilitate seamless transactions and services for their customers. This could involve creating digital wallets or platforms that can interact with CBDCs, enabling customers to manage their digital and traditional currencies in one place.

- **Focus on Customer Education and Support:** In the CBDC era, banks have an important role in educating and supporting their customers through the transition. Many customers may be unfamiliar or uncomfortable with digital currencies and the associated technologies. Banks can offer educational resources, workshops, and personalized support to help customers navigate these new financial tools, thereby strengthening customer trust and loyalty.

- **Regulatory Compliance and Advocacy:** Banks will need to navigate the regulatory landscape that comes with CBDCs, which may involve new laws and guidelines. Staying compliant will be crucial, but banks can also play a role in advocating for regulations that support innovation while protecting consumer interests.

For traditional banks, the rise of CBDCs represents both a challenge and an opportunity. By embracing new technologies, forming strategic partnerships, and rethinking their service offerings, banks can transform these challenges into opportunities for growth and innovation. In doing so, they can ensure their continued relevance and success in a financial world that is becoming increasingly digital and decentralized. The future of banking in the age of CBDCs is not just about adapting to change – it's about leading it.

Chapter 9
Decentralized vs. Centralized Digital Currencies

Fundamental Differences and Philosophical Underpinnings

The debate between decentralized currencies and Central Bank Digital Currencies (CBDCs) is not just about technology — it's a clash of fundamentally different philosophies and design principles underpinning the future of money.

- **Autonomy vs. Control:** Decentralized currencies like Bitcoin were born out of a desire for financial autonomy and a distrust of centralized financial institutions. They embody a philosophy of freedom from central control, offering a peer-to-peer system where transactions are verified by a distributed network. This structure ensures that no single entity, be it a government or financial institution, can control or manipulate the currency. In contrast, CBDCs are designed as an extension of state monetary policy into the digital world. They represent a digital form of a country's fiat currency, controlled and issued by the central bank. This central control allows governments to maintain traditional monetary policy tools in a digital format, like adjusting interest rates or controlling money supply.

- **Design Principles:** The design principles of decentralized currencies revolve around security, transparency, and immutability. Transactions on a blockchain are transparent and irreversible, creating a trustless system where users don't need to trust each other but can rely on the technology itself. CBDCs, on the other hand, are designed with different priorities, such as integration with existing financial systems, ease of use, and regulatory compliance. While they may use blockchain or other forms of DLT (Distributed Ledger Technology), they are typically permissioned systems where the central bank has ultimate control.

- **Philosophical Underpinnings:** The philosophical underpinnings of decentralized currencies can be traced back to libertarian ideals, emphasizing individual freedom, privacy, and resistance to censorship. Decentralized currencies are seen as a way to reduce the power of central authorities and give more control to individuals over their financial dealings. Conversely, CBDCs are rooted in a more traditional view of money and banking, where central authorities are responsible for maintaining financial stability, controlling inflation, and ensuring the smooth functioning of the financial system.

- **Use Cases and Adoption:** The use cases of decentralized currencies often focus on providing an alternative to traditional banking, especially in areas lacking financial infrastructure or in situations where trust in government or banks is low. They have also become popular as a speculative asset and a hedge against inflation. CBDCs, however, are designed to complement and enhance the existing financial system, offering a digital alternative to cash that is stable, reliable, and regulated. They aim to streamline payments, increase efficiency, and potentially bring financial services to underserved populations.

- **Privacy and Surveillance:** A key difference lies in privacy and surveillance. Decentralized currencies offer a degree of anonymity and privacy, though not absolute, as transactions are recorded on a public ledger. CBDCs, however, could enable governments to monitor and analyze financial transactions at an unprecedented scale, raising concerns about privacy and the potential for surveillance.

In summary, the contrast between decentralized currencies and CBDCs highlights a fundamental divergence in how the future of money is envisioned. One path leads towards a more decentralized, autonomous financial world, while the other reinforces the role of central authorities in the digital age. As we move forward, the coexistence and interplay between these two models will shape not just our financial systems, but the very nature of economic freedom and control in the digital era. The future of money, it seems, will be a tale of two currencies – each with its vision, strengths, and challenges.

Operational Mechanisms and Efficiency

In the dynamic world of digital currencies, the operational mechanisms driving decentralized currencies and Central Bank Digital Currencies (CBDCs) present a stark contrast in efficiency and technology implementation. This section delves deep into these mechanisms, laying bare the intricate workings and efficiencies of both systems.

- **Decentralized Currencies: Blockchain at the Core:** Decentralized currencies, like Bitcoin and Ethereum, operate on the revolutionary technology of blockchain. This distributed ledger technology is the backbone of their operational mechanism. It's a series of interconnected blocks, each securely containing transaction data, linked chronologically in a chain. What makes this system so efficient and unique is its inherent design:

  - **Peer-to-Peer Transactions:** Decentralized currencies facilitate direct transactions between users, eliminating the need for intermediaries like banks. This peer-to-peer model greatly reduces transaction times and fees, making it a swift and cost-effective solution.

  - **Transparency and Security:** Every transaction on the blockchain is transparent and publicly verifiable. While this ensures transparency, it also adds a layer of security. The immutable nature of blockchain means once a transaction is recorded, it cannot be altered or deleted, which significantly reduces fraud and error.

  - **Decentralization:** There's no central point of control in a blockchain. The distributed nature means that the ledger is maintained across thousands of computers, making it incredibly resilient to attacks and system failures.

- **Consensus Mechanisms:** Blockchain uses consensus mechanisms like Proof of Work (PoW) or Proof of Stake (PoS) to validate transactions. These mechanisms ensure that only legitimate transactions are added to the blockchain, further bolstering the trustworthiness of the system.

- **CBDCs: A Blend of Old and New:** CBDCs, on the other hand, represent a fusion of traditional banking principles with modern digital technology. They are issued and regulated by a country's central bank and may use a mix of traditional banking infrastructure and blockchain technology.

- **Centralized Control:** Unlike decentralized currencies, CBDCs are centrally controlled. This centralization allows central banks to implement monetary policies directly through the digital currency. However, it also means that CBDCs lack the same level of resistance to censorship and control that decentralized currencies boast.

- **Efficiency in Traditional Systems:** CBDCs aim to streamline traditional financial systems, making transactions faster and more efficient compared to conventional banking methods. They can reduce the need for intermediaries in some processes, though not to the extent of decentralized systems.

- **Hybrid Blockchain Models:** Some CBDCs may employ private or permissioned blockchains, where access to the ledger is controlled by the issuing authority. This can provide some benefits of blockchain, such as traceability and security, but within a controlled environment.

- **Interoperability Challenges:** CBDCs need to seamlessly integrate with existing financial systems, which presents a significant challenge. They must be designed to work within the complex web of global finance, from retail banking to international trade.

When it comes to operational efficiency, decentralized currencies excel in reducing transaction costs and times, thanks to their elimination of intermediaries and their global, borderless nature. However, they face challenges in terms of scalability and energy consumption, especially those using PoW mechanisms.

CBDCs, while more efficient than traditional banking systems, may not match the speed and low cost of decentralized currencies. Their efficiency gains are more about enhancing the existing financial systems, providing a digital complement to cash, and facilitating better implementation of monetary policies.

In summary, while decentralized currencies and CBDCs both venture into the realm of digital finance, they operate on very different principles. Decentralized currencies champion autonomy and peer-to-peer efficiency, leveraging the full power of blockchain technology. CBDCs, meanwhile, represent an evolution of traditional finance, seeking to modernize and streamline existing structures with a touch of blockchain innovation. Each has its unique strengths and challenges, painting a diverse picture of the future of digital currency.

User Autonomy and Privacy Concerns

As we delve into the realm of digital currencies, the contrast between user autonomy and privacy in decentralized versus centralized digital currencies becomes starkly evident. This segment thoroughly examines these implications, offering a comprehensive view of how both forms of digital currency impact the individual's control over their financial transactions and personal data.

-   **Decentralized Currencies: A Haven for Privacy and Autonomy:** At the heart of decentralized digital currencies like Bitcoin and Ethereum lies a profound commitment to user autonomy and privacy. These currencies are built on blockchain technology, a decentralized network that upholds the principles of anonymity and user sovereignty. Here's how they safeguard these aspects:

- **Anonymity in Transactions:** Decentralized currencies typically allow users to conduct transactions without revealing their identities. While the transaction details are recorded on the blockchain, the parties involved are often represented by pseudonyms or cryptographic addresses.

- **User Control Over Funds:** In the decentralized ecosystem, users have complete control over their digital wallets. They can manage their funds without any intervention from central authorities, banks, or governments. This control extends to how, when, and where they choose to spend or invest their digital assets.

- **Reduced Surveillance:** Without a central body overseeing transactions, decentralized currencies inherently resist surveillance. This lack of oversight is a double-edged sword; while it protects user privacy, it also opens avenues for illicit activities. However, the focus remains on empowering users with privacy in their financial dealings.

- **Privacy-focused Alternatives:** Some decentralized currencies, like Monero and Zcash, take privacy a step further. They employ advanced cryptographic techniques to obscure transaction details, offering an even higher level of privacy and anonymity.

- **Centralized Digital Currencies: The Privacy Paradox:** Central Bank Digital Currencies (CBDCs), representing a centralized form of digital currency, present a different narrative in terms of user privacy and autonomy. While they bring digital efficiency to traditional currency systems, they also raise concerns about state surveillance and data privacy:

- **Potential for Surveillance:** Given their centralized nature, CBDCs could enable governments to monitor and analyze financial transactions closely. This capability could lead to a scenario where state entities have access to detailed records of individual spending patterns, transactions, and financial behaviors.

- **Data Collection and Privacy Risks:** The implementation of CBDCs may involve the collection of personal data for identity verification and transaction processing. This raises concerns about the security of this data, the potential for breaches, and the misuse of personal information.

- **Government Control Over Transactions:** CBDCs could allow governments to exercise control over how and where money is spent. This could manifest in the blocking of transactions to certain entities or for specific purposes, which would significantly curtail user autonomy in financial matters.

- **Dependence on State Policies:** The privacy and autonomy of users in a CBDC-led system would largely depend on the policies and regulations set by the issuing government. This dependence could lead to varying degrees of financial freedom and privacy across different countries.

In conclusion, the journey into the future of digital currencies is a balancing act between technological innovation and the preservation of user privacy and autonomy. While decentralized currencies offer a realm of privacy and user control, they come with their own set of challenges. On the other hand, CBDCs, while streamlining financial transactions under a centralized system, raise significant concerns about privacy and state control.

The path forward requires a nuanced understanding of these technologies and their implications. It calls for regulations that safeguard user privacy while leveraging the benefits of digital currencies. As we forge ahead in this digital age, the discourse around user autonomy and privacy in the context of digital currencies will undoubtedly continue to evolve, shaping the contours of our financial freedom and rights in the digital era.

Financial Inclusion and Accessibility

The dawn of digital currencies, both decentralized and centralized, opens new avenues in addressing the age-old issue of financial inclusion. This section delves deep into how these two forms of digital money – decentralized currencies like Bitcoin and Central Bank Digital Currencies (CBDCs) – approach the critical mission of making financial services accessible to all, especially those who have been traditionally excluded from the financial system.

Decentralized Currencies: Bridging the Gap for the Unbanked: Decentralized digital currencies have emerged as potential game-changers for financial inclusion. Their unique characteristics offer several advantages:

- **Lowering Barriers to Entry:** Unlike traditional banking systems that often require extensive documentation, credit history checks, and minimum balance requirements, decentralized currencies provide a more straightforward entry point. With just a smartphone and internet access, individuals can create a digital wallet and participate in the global economy.

- **Empowering the Unbanked:** In many developing regions, access to banking facilities is limited. Decentralized currencies bypass the need for physical banking infrastructure, allowing people in the most remote areas to engage in financial activities like saving, investing, and transferring funds.

- **Reducing Transaction Costs:** High fees for basic financial services are a significant barrier in traditional banking, particularly for low-income individuals. Decentralized currencies, by eliminating intermediaries, often result in significantly lower transaction fees.

- **Promoting Financial Autonomy:** Decentralized currencies empower users with control over their funds, free from governmental or institutional oversight. This autonomy is especially crucial for those in politically unstable or inflation-prone regions.

CBDCs: Integrating Financial Inclusion into the Existing Framework: CBDCs, while being a centralized form of digital currency, also hold promise in enhancing financial inclusion:

- **Structured Integration into Financial Systems:** Being issued by central banks, CBDCs can be seamlessly integrated into the existing financial framework. This integration means they can leverage the current infrastructure to reach a wider population effectively.

- **Regulatory Assurance:** The backing of central banks potentially makes CBDCs more stable and reliable compared to some decentralized options. This stability can build trust among potential users who are hesitant about the relatively volatile nature of certain decentralized currencies.

- **Programmable Features for Inclusion:** CBDCs can be designed with programmable features that target specific financial inclusion goals. For instance, they could be used to distribute welfare payments directly to the intended recipients, reducing leakage and ensuring that aid reaches those in need.

- **Overcoming Digital Divide Challenges:** While CBDCs rely on digital infrastructure, central banks can implement policies and partner with local institutions to overcome challenges such as limited internet access or lack of digital literacy, thus extending financial services to traditionally underserved communities.

While both decentralized currencies and CBDCs offer significant potential for financial inclusion, their approaches and challenges are distinct. Decentralized currencies shine in providing autonomy and reducing entry barriers, while CBDCs bring stability and structured integration into the current financial system. However, the success of both in achieving financial inclusion will depend on various factors, including technological advancements, regulatory environments, and the global socio-economic landscape.

In envisioning the future, one can speculate that a hybrid model might emerge, where the autonomy and efficiency of decentralized currencies complement the stability and structured integration of CBDCs. This synergy could create a more inclusive and accessible financial system, one where the benefits of digital currency innovation are enjoyed by people from all walks of life.

As we ponder over this possibility, it's essential to keep in mind the ultimate goal: a financial system that serves everyone, not just the privileged few. The journey towards this goal with digital currencies, both decentralized and centralized, is one filled with potential and promises, paving the way for a more inclusive financial future.

Security Features and Vulnerabilities

In the evolving landscape of digital currencies, understanding the security features and potential vulnerabilities of decentralized currencies compared to Central Bank Digital Currencies (CBDCs) is crucial. This section delves into the intricate world of digital currency security, contrasting the strengths and weaknesses of both decentralized and centralized systems.

- **Decentralized Currencies: Strengths and Weaknesses:** Decentralized digital currencies like Bitcoin and Ethereum are built on blockchain technology, a distributed ledger that offers several unique security advantages:

- **Decentralized Control:** The absence of a central authority in decentralized currencies reduces the risk of systemic failure. The blockchain is maintained by a network of nodes, making it resilient to single points of failure.

- **Cryptography:** Transactions in decentralized currencies are secured using advanced cryptographic techniques. Each transaction is encrypted and linked to the previous transaction, creating a chain that is incredibly difficult to alter.

- **Transparency and Immutability:** Every transaction is recorded on a public ledger, offering transparency. Once added, the data cannot be changed, which significantly reduces the risk of fraud.

However, decentralized currencies also have vulnerabilities:

- **Dependence on Technology:** The security of decentralized currencies heavily relies on technology – both hardware and software. Vulnerabilities in protocol design or implementation can be exploited.

- **User Responsibility:** Users are responsible for their private keys. Lost or stolen keys can lead to irreversible loss of funds, and there is no central authority to appeal to in such cases.

- **Scalability and Network Congestion:** As the network grows, scalability issues can lead to network congestion, potentially making the system slower and more susceptible to certain types of attacks.

- **CBDCs: A Different Security Paradigm:** CBDCs, being centralized, offer a different security approach:

1. **Centralized Oversight:** CBDCs are regulated and overseen by central banks, providing a layer of security and trust. These entities can implement and enforce robust cybersecurity measures.

2. **Contingency and Recovery Plans:** Central banks can deploy comprehensive contingency plans for system failures, including backups and recovery protocols, which can be more challenging in a decentralized environment.

3. **Regulatory Compliance:** CBDCs can ensure compliance with existing financial regulations, including anti-money laundering (AML) and combating the financing of terrorism (CFT) standards.

However, CBDCs also face significant security challenges:

1. **Target for Cyberattacks:** As centralized systems, CBDCs could become prime targets for cyberattacks. A successful attack on a central bank's digital currency system could have far-reaching consequences.

2. **Privacy and Surveillance:** While offering security, the centralized nature of CBDCs raises concerns about user privacy and potential government surveillance.

3. **Infrastructure Reliability:** The reliance on a centralized technological infrastructure means that any failure in the system could have widespread implications for all users of the CBDC.

The resilience of decentralized currencies lies in their distributed nature, making them less vulnerable to single points of failure. Conversely, CBDCs can leverage centralized control for rapid response and recovery in the event of an incident.

In summary, while decentralized currencies offer high security through cryptography and distributed consensus, they place much of the responsibility on the user and face scalability challenges. CBDCs, on the other hand, provide the security of regulatory oversight and centralized control but raise concerns about privacy and potential systemic risks.

As we ponder these security paradigms, it's crucial to consider that the future might see the coexistence of both systems, each addressing unique needs in the digital currency ecosystem. The ongoing development in both arenas promises a future where the strengths of one complement the weaknesses of the other, leading to a more secure and robust global financial system.

Regulatory and Legal Frameworks

In the world of digital currencies, the regulatory and legal landscape forms a complex and ever-evolving puzzle. This is particularly true when contrasting decentralized currencies with state-issued Central Bank Digital Currencies (CBDCs). Let's delve into the intricate regulatory challenges and legal frameworks that govern these two distinct realms of digital finance.

- **Global Regulatory Landscape:** The global regulatory landscape for digital currencies is as diverse as it is fragmented. Different countries have adopted varying approaches to regulating these new financial assets.

  - **Decentralized Currencies:** Decentralized currencies like Bitcoin and Ethereum operate in a largely unregulated space. However, countries are increasingly trying to fit them into existing financial regulatory frameworks. This includes measures for anti-money laundering (AML), combating the financing of terrorism (CFT), and investor protection. Some countries, like Japan, have embraced these currencies, providing clear guidelines and regulatory frameworks. In contrast, others like China have taken a more restrictive approach, banning cryptocurrency exchanges and ICOs.

  - **CBDCs:** As state-issued digital currencies, CBDCs fall directly under the regulatory purview of their issuing central banks and financial authorities. They are designed to comply with existing financial laws and regulations. However, the introduction of CBDCs also necessitates new legal frameworks to address issues unique to digital currencies, such as digital identity verification, data protection, and cross-border transaction rules.

- **Regulating Decentralized Currencies:** The decentralized nature of cryptocurrencies poses significant regulatory challenges:

  - **Lack of Central Control:** Without a central authority, enforcing regulatory compliance is challenging. Decentralized networks operate on a global scale, often beyond the reach of any single country's jurisdiction.

  - **Anonymity and Privacy:** The pseudo-anonymous nature of transactions in many decentralized currencies complicates efforts to implement traditional AML and CFT regulations.

  - **Innovative Technology:** The rapidly evolving technology underpinning these currencies often outpaces regulatory developments, leading to a regulatory lag.

- **Legal Implications of CBDCs:** CBDCs, in contrast, bring a different set of legal considerations:

  - **Monetary Sovereignty:** CBDCs reaffirm a nation's monetary sovereignty in the digital age. They represent a digital extension of the state's currency and are thus subject to the same legal tender laws as traditional fiat currencies.

  - **Privacy vs. Surveillance:** CBDCs raise important legal questions about privacy and state surveillance. How much transactional data should central banks collect and store? What safeguards should be in place to protect individual privacy rights?

  - **Cross-Border Transactions:** CBDCs could potentially revolutionize cross-border transactions. However, this raises complex legal questions regarding jurisdiction, foreign exchange regulations, and international trade laws.

As we explore these regulatory and legal frameworks, it's important to ask: "How can a balance be struck between innovation and regulation in the digital currency space?" and "What legal protections should be afforded to users of both decentralized currencies and CBDCs?"

In conclusion, navigating the regulatory and legal landscape of digital currencies requires a delicate balance. For decentralized currencies, the challenge lies in imposing regulatory oversight without stifling innovation. For CBDCs, the challenge is to integrate them into the existing financial system while addressing new legal issues they bring forth. This journey is not just about creating rules and laws but about shaping the future of finance in a way that is safe, equitable, and forward-looking.

Impact on Global Economic Dynamics

The emergence of digital currencies, both decentralized and centralized (CBDCs), heralds a new era in global economics. Their influence extends far beyond mere financial transactions, affecting international trade, currency valuation, and power dynamics. Let's delve into this intricate tapestry of economic change.

International Trade

- **Decentralized Currencies:** Decentralized currencies like Bitcoin have the potential to revolutionize international trade. By bypassing traditional banking channels, they offer a faster, cheaper, and more efficient means of conducting cross-border transactions. For businesses, this means reduced costs and increased speed in international trade dealings. However, the volatility of these currencies presents a risk, potentially impacting pricing and contract stability.

- **CBDCs:** The introduction of CBDCs can streamline international trade by offering a stable, government-backed digital currency option. They could reduce the need for currency conversion, lower transaction costs, and speed up settlement times. However, the success of CBDCs in international trade largely depends on their acceptance and interoperability between different countries' digital currencies.

Currency Valuation

- **Market Forces vs. State Control:** Decentralized currencies are subject to market forces, with their value determined by supply and demand dynamics. This contrasts with CBDCs, where value is pegged to the issuing country's fiat currency and controlled by monetary policy.

- **Impact on Fiat Currencies:** The rise of digital currencies could lead to a diminished role for traditional fiat currencies in global finance. As more people adopt digital currencies for trade and investment, the demand for traditional currencies might decrease, potentially affecting their value.

Shift in Power Dynamics

- **From State to Individual:** Decentralized currencies represent a shift in financial power from state to individual. They offer individuals more control over their financial assets, free from government intervention or banking oversight. This could lead to a more democratized financial system, where individuals have greater freedom in how they store, spend, and invest their money.

- **State-Issued Digital Currencies:** On the other hand, CBDCs reinforce state control over currency. They represent an extension of state monetary policy into the digital realm, potentially increasing governmental oversight and control over financial transactions.

As we explore these impacts, consider the following questions: "How might the widespread adoption of digital currencies reshape the global economic landscape?" and "What are the potential risks and benefits of moving towards a digital currency-dominated world?"

In conclusion, the rise of digital currencies, whether decentralized or centralized, signals a significant transformation in global economic dynamics. While they offer the promise of more efficient and inclusive financial systems, they also present challenges in terms of volatility, regulatory oversight, and the balance of power. The future of global economics in this digital age is not just a story of technological advancement but also one of adaptation, regulation, and the ongoing quest for economic stability and fairness.

Chapter 10
Looking Ahead: Challenges and Opportunities

Advancements in Blockchain Technology

As we peer into the future of blockchain technology, we find ourselves at the cusp of remarkable transformations. This chapter delves deep into the upcoming trends in blockchain, each poised to further revolutionize the landscape of decentralized finance.

Energy-Efficient Consensus Mechanisms

- **The Green Revolution in Blockchain:** Traditional Proof of Work (PoW) mechanisms, as used in Bitcoin, are known for their high energy consumption. The new wave in blockchain development focuses on more energy-efficient consensus mechanisms like Proof of Stake (PoS), Delegated Proof of Stake (DPoS), and others. These mechanisms promise significant reductions in energy usage, thereby addressing environmental concerns.

- **Real-World Impact:** The adoption of these energy-efficient mechanisms is not just about saving energy; it's a move towards a more sustainable and socially responsible blockchain ecosystem. This shift could lead to broader acceptance of blockchain technology, especially among environmentally conscious investors and users.

Enhanced Scalability Solutions

- **Layer-Two Protocols:** Scalability remains a critical challenge for blockchain networks. Layer-two protocols, like Lightning Network for Bitcoin or Plasma and Rollups for Ethereum, are emerging solutions. These protocols operate on top of the blockchain and enable faster, cheaper transactions without compromising the security of the main chain.

- **Implications for Decentralized Finance:** Enhanced scalability directly translates into more efficient and accessible decentralized finance (DeFi) services. With faster transaction speeds and lower fees, DeFi could become more appealing for mainstream financial applications, widening its adoption.

Integration of Quantum-Resistant Algorithms

- **Quantum Threat to Blockchain:** The advent of quantum computing poses a new kind of threat to blockchain technology, as traditional cryptographic algorithms could potentially be broken by quantum computers. This scenario necessitates the integration of quantum-resistant algorithms into blockchain systems.

- **Future-Proofing Blockchain:** Developing and integrating these algorithms is crucial for the longevity and security of blockchain networks. By preemptively adapting to quantum threats, blockchain technology can remain a secure foundation for digital assets and transactions in the post-quantum world.

Consider this: "How do you think these advancements in blockchain technology will shape the future of digital finance?" This question invites readers to contemplate the broader implications of these technological strides, especially in how they might democratize and secure financial systems worldwide.

In conclusion, the future of blockchain technology is not just a tale of technical advancements but a journey towards more sustainable, scalable, and secure financial systems. These upcoming trends in blockchain, from green consensus mechanisms to quantum-resistant algorithms, are set to redefine the landscape of decentralized finance, paving the way for a more inclusive, efficient, and resilient financial ecosystem. As we look ahead, it's clear that blockchain technology will continue to be a dynamic and transformative force in the world of finance.

AI's Evolving Role in Financial Services

The world of finance is on the brink of a transformative era, largely driven by the rapid evolution of artificial intelligence (AI). As we venture into the future, AI's role in financial services is expected to expand significantly, bringing about groundbreaking changes in how financial systems operate and how they serve individuals and businesses.

Advancements in Predictive Analytics

- **Predictive Power Unleashed:** AI's capability in predictive analytics is set to reach new heights. Leveraging massive datasets, AI will not just react to market trends but anticipate them, offering forecasts with unprecedented accuracy. This includes predicting market fluctuations, consumer behavior, and potential financial crises.

- **Real-World Applications:** In practical terms, these advancements mean that investors, both large and small, can make more informed decisions. For instance, an AI system could analyze global economic indicators to predict stock market trends, helping investors to strategize their portfolio allocations more effectively.

Personalized Financial Advice

- **AI as a Personal Financial Advisor:** AI will play an increasingly personalized role in financial advice. Going beyond robo-advisors, AI systems will offer tailor-made financial guidance, considering an individual's financial goals, risk tolerance, and life stage.

- **Impact on Personal Finance Management:** This personalized advice could revolutionize personal finance management. Imagine an AI that not only advises on investments but also helps in budgeting, identifies saving opportunities, and even suggests insurance products based on personal lifestyle and needs.

AI in Decentralized Finance Data Ecosystems

- **Managing Complex Data:** Decentralized finance (DeFi) is characterized by its complex, expansive data ecosystems. AI's role in managing and making sense of this data will be crucial. It will analyze patterns across various blockchain platforms, identify opportunities for arbitrage, and detect early signs of fraudulent activities.

- **Enhancing DeFi Efficiency and Security:** AI's analytical prowess can significantly enhance the efficiency and security of DeFi platforms. It can automate and optimize liquidity pools, predict market movements for better yield farming strategies, and enhance the security of smart contracts by identifying vulnerabilities.

Consider pondering over, "How might AI-driven personalized financial advice change your approach to money management?" or "In what ways do you think AI could safeguard your investments in the volatile world of DeFi?" These questions encourage readers to reflect on the personal impact of AI's advancements in finance.

In summary, AI's evolving role in financial services is poised to redefine the financial landscape. From advanced predictive analytics and personalized financial advice to managing complex data in decentralized finance, AI is set to become an indispensable tool in the financial toolkit. As we look to the future, the synergy of AI and finance promises not only heightened efficiency and security but also a more intuitive and personalized financial experience for users around the globe. The horizon of AI in finance is vast and exciting, holding the potential to democratize financial expertise and empower individuals in their financial journeys like never before.

Regulatory Evolution and Global Standards in Digital Currencies

As we navigate the complex and rapidly evolving landscape of digital currencies, the need for an effective and cohesive global regulatory framework becomes increasingly apparent. The future of digital currency regulation, be it for decentralized cryptocurrencies or centralized digital currencies (CBDCs), is teetering at a crossroads, facing challenges and opportunities that could redefine the financial world.

The Challenge of Global Regulatory Cohesion

- **Diverse Regulatory Approaches:** The foremost challenge lies in the diversity of regulatory approaches across different nations. Countries vary vastly in their financial policies, economic stability, technological advancement, and legal systems. This variance has led to a mosaic of regulations that range from outright bans of cryptocurrencies in some regions to welcoming regulatory environments in others.

- **Seeking Common Ground:** The quest for common ground in regulations is a complex but necessary endeavor. The interconnected nature of the global economy means that inconsistency in regulations can lead to loopholes, fraud, and systemic risks. A coherent set of global standards is needed to ensure stability, fairness, and security in the digital currency landscape.

Future Regulatory Scenarios

- **Harmonization of Laws Across Borders:** One potential scenario involves the harmonization of digital currency laws across national boundaries. This could manifest as international treaties or agreements, much like the Basel Accords in banking. Such harmonization would aim to create a level playing field, reduce opportunities for regulatory arbitrage, and promote global cooperation in monitoring and regulating digital currencies.

- **Balancing Innovation and Consumer Protection:** The delicate balance between fostering innovation and protecting consumers will be a crucial aspect of future regulatory frameworks. On one hand, overregulation could stifle the growth and potential benefits of digital currencies. On the other, insufficient regulation could expose consumers and the financial system to significant risks.

- **Role of International Organizations:** International organizations such as the IMF, World Bank, and various UN agencies might play a pivotal role in shaping these global standards. Their involvement could ensure that both developed and developing countries have a say in the regulatory process, promoting inclusivity and fairness.

- **Adapting to Technological Advancements:** As technology evolves, so must the regulations. Future frameworks will need to be flexible and adaptive, capable of responding to new developments like quantum computing, which could disrupt current cryptographic standards, or the advent of new forms of digital assets.

In summary, the regulatory evolution in the realm of digital currencies is a journey marked by complexity, necessity, and immense potential. As we look towards the future, the development of a cohesive global regulatory framework stands as both a challenge and an opportunity – one that calls for international cooperation, foresight, and a fine-tuned balance between embracing technological advancements and safeguarding the financial system. The path ahead is uncharted, but with thoughtful navigation, it holds the promise of a more stable, inclusive, and innovative financial future.

The Intersection of Finance with Emerging Technologies

In the ever-evolving world of finance, the convergence of blockchain and AI with other cutting-edge technologies like the Internet of Things (IoT) and 5G networks is opening new horizons for financial innovation. This intersection is not just a fusion of technologies; it represents a profound shift in how financial services are conceptualized, delivered, and experienced.

Integrating Blockchain and AI with IoT and 5G

- **Blockchain and IoT for Enhanced Transparency:** The integration of blockchain with IoT is transforming asset management and tracking. Imagine a world where every item, from a container in a cargo ship to a bottle of wine in your cellar, is connected to an IoT device that records real-time data on a blockchain. This would ensure unparalleled traceability and transparency, significantly reducing fraud and improving supply chain efficiency.

- **AI and IoT for Personalized Financial Services:** AI's analytical prowess combined with IoT's data-gathering capabilities can revolutionize personalized financial services. For instance, IoT devices in smart homes or vehicles could provide data that AI algorithms use to offer customized insurance policies or investment advice, tailored to the user's lifestyle and habits.

- **5G's Role in Accelerating Financial Transactions:** The introduction of 5G networks promises to significantly boost the speed and efficiency of financial transactions. With higher data speeds and reduced latency, 5G will enhance the performance of blockchain networks, enable faster AI processing, and improve the responsiveness of IoT devices, leading to real-time financial interactions.

Potential for New Financial Products and Services

- **Smart Contracts in IoT Environments:** The use of smart contracts in IoT environments could automate a range of financial transactions. For example, a smart vehicle could automatically process lease payments, insurance, and even parking fees, based on real-time usage data and predefined smart contract conditions.

- **Decentralized Finance (DeFi) Meets IoT:** As DeFi continues to grow, its integration with IoT could see the development of novel financial products. Imagine IoT devices acting as autonomous economic agents, engaging in financial transactions, and even participating in DeFi protocols independently.

- **Enhanced Risk Management and Underwriting:** The combination of AI, blockchain, and IoT data can vastly improve risk management and underwriting processes in finance. Insurers could leverage this integrated technology to assess risks more accurately and dynamically, leading to more efficient pricing models and policies.

- **New Avenues in Banking:** Banks could utilize these technologies to offer innovative services, such as IoT-enabled mobile banking, AI-driven financial advisory, and blockchain-based secure transactions. This could redefine the banking experience, making it more integrated with customers' daily lives.

In conclusion, the fusion of blockchain and AI with emerging technologies like IoT and 5G is not just reshaping the financial landscape; it's creating it anew. The potential for new financial products and services arising from this convergence is immense, promising a future where finance is more integrated, personalized, and efficient. As we stand at the cusp of this technological revolution, the possibilities are as boundless as our imagination, beckoning us towards an exciting and uncharted future in the world of finance.

Impact on Traditional Financial Institutions and Systems

The rise of digital currencies is not just a technological evolution; it's a catalyst for a complete transformation of traditional financial institutions and systems. As we sail into this new era, let's explore how established banks and financial entities are gearing up to adapt to the digital currency wave.

Redefining Banking in the Digital Age

- **Embracing Digital Transformation:** Traditional banks are increasingly embracing digital transformation. This involves not just digitizing existing services, but fundamentally rethinking banking operations. Banks are integrating digital wallets, introducing online platforms for loans and investments, and leveraging blockchain for secure and efficient transactions.

- **Cultural Shift in Banking:** There's a cultural shift underway in these institutions. Banks are moving from being conservative entities to dynamic, technology-driven organizations. This shift is not just in services but in mindset, where agility, customer-centricity, and innovation become the core values.

Collaborative Synergies with Fintech Companies

- **Partnership Models:** The future will likely see more partnerships between traditional banks and fintech companies. These partnerships can range from using fintech platforms for better customer engagement to co-creating new financial products that combine the trust and scale of traditional banking with the agility and innovation of fintech.

- **Learning from Fintech:** Banks are also learning from fintech companies. This includes adopting lean operational models, using data analytics for personalized services, and embracing mobile-first strategies to meet the expectations of the digital-savvy generation.

Transformation of Traditional Banking Models

- **From Brick-and-Mortar to Digital-First:** The traditional brick-and-mortar banking model is undergoing a transformation. Banks are reducing their physical branches and investing in robust digital channels, offering everything from digital account opening to virtual customer service.

- **Innovative Financial Products:** As digital currencies gain prominence, banks are exploring innovative financial products. This includes digital currency-based savings accounts, investment products, and even crypto-linked loans.

Navigating Regulatory Challenges

- **Compliance and Adaptation:** Banks are navigating the complex regulatory landscape that comes with digital currencies. This involves not only complying with existing financial regulations but also adapting to new rules that govern digital assets and transactions.

Anticipating Customer Needs

- **Customer-Centric Approaches:** Banks are focusing on anticipating and meeting customer needs in a digital-first environment. This means offering personalized financial advice, seamless cross-platform experiences, and ensuring security and privacy in digital transactions.

In conclusion, traditional financial institutions and systems are at a pivotal juncture. The rise of digital currencies is not just a challenge to be met but an opportunity to redefine banking itself. As these institutions adapt and evolve, they are poised to offer a blend of reliability, innovation, and efficiency, aligning with the changing face of global currency and customer expectations in the digital age. The future of banking, in this context, appears not just digital but dynamic, customer-focused, and more inclusive than ever before.

Social and Economic Impacts of Decentralized Finance

The advent of decentralized finance (DeFi) is not just a technological breakthrough; it's a socio-economic revolution in the making. As we turn the pages towards a future where DeFi becomes mainstream, let's dissect the multifaceted social and economic impacts this paradigm shift might bring.

Financial Inclusion: A Gateway to Empowerment

- **Reaching the Unbanked:** One of the most profound impacts of DeFi is its potential to reach the unbanked and underbanked populations. By removing the need for traditional banking infrastructure and simplifying financial transactions, DeFi stands to offer financial services to millions who are currently excluded from the financial system.

- **Case Studies:** Consider examples like a farmer in a remote village using a DeFi platform for a microloan or a small business owner in an emerging economy accessing global markets through cryptocurrency. These stories highlight how DeFi can democratize financial access.

Bridging the Income Inequality Gap

- **Economic Empowerment:** DeFi could play a significant role in bridging the income inequality gap. By providing equal access to financial tools and investment opportunities, it empowers individuals to grow their wealth, irrespective of their geographical location or socio-economic background.

- **Crowdfunding and Entrepreneurship:** DeFi enables crowdfunding and peer-to-peer lending, offering a new avenue for entrepreneurs to raise capital. This fosters innovation and drives economic growth, particularly in developing economies where traditional funding sources are scarce.

Shifting Global Economic Power Dynamics

- **Decentralizing Economic Power:** DeFi has the potential to decentralize economic power. By allowing seamless global transactions and reducing dependency on traditional banking systems, it can shift economic power from traditional financial hubs to a more distributed model.

- **Impact on International Trade:** DeFi can simplify cross-border transactions, reducing costs and increasing efficiency. This has implications for international trade, potentially making it more accessible and equitable for smaller players.

Societal Implications of Financial Autonomy

- **Enhanced Financial Literacy:** The rise of DeFi will likely lead to increased financial literacy as individuals take more control over their financial assets. This empowerment comes with the responsibility of understanding complex financial instruments and risks.

- **Community and Social Structures:** DeFi could foster new forms of community and social structures around finance. Decentralized autonomous organizations (DAOs), for instance, represent a new way of collective decision-making and resource allocation.

In conclusion, as DeFi continues to evolve, its potential social and economic impacts are vast and varied. From financial inclusion and empowerment to reshaping global economic dynamics, DeFi promises a future where financial services are more accessible, equitable, and aligned with the needs of a digitally connected world. However, this future also demands a responsible and informed approach to leveraging these technologies, ensuring that the benefits of DeFi extend across all strata of society, bridging gaps rather than widening them. As we embark on this journey, the narrative of DeFi remains one of hope, challenges, and immense possibilities, painting a picture of a more inclusive and empowered global financial landscape.

Challenges in Maintaining Security and Privacy

In the realm of decentralized financial systems, the twin pillars of security and privacy are constantly under siege from evolving threats. As we peer into the future, it becomes crucial to understand and anticipate these challenges to safeguard the integrity of decentralized finance (DeFi).

The Evolving Landscape of Cyber Threats

- **Sophisticated Cyber Attacks:** The digital nature of decentralized finance makes it a ripe target for cybercriminals. Future threats are likely to become more sophisticated, employing advanced techniques like AI-powered hacking, deep fakes in identity theft, and quantum computing to break encryption.

- **Case Studies:** Consider incidents like the DAO hack or the numerous DeFi platform breaches that have resulted in substantial losses. These examples underscore the need for robust security protocols in decentralized systems.

Privacy: A Balancing Act

- **Surveillance vs. Anonymity:** As regulatory bodies strive to clamp down on illicit activities, the tension between surveillance and user anonymity intensifies. Future DeFi platforms may need to navigate this delicate balance, ensuring user privacy while complying with regulatory requirements like Anti-Money Laundering (AML) and Know Your Customer (KYC) norms.

- **Emerging Privacy Solutions:** Discuss innovations like zero-knowledge proofs and private smart contracts that promise enhanced privacy without compromising regulatory compliance.

Regulatory Compliance: A Double-Edged Sword

- **Global Regulatory Variance:** The lack of a unified regulatory framework for DeFi presents a significant challenge. Future systems will need to adapt to diverse regulations across jurisdictions, complicating the compliance landscape.

- **Impact on Innovation:** While regulation is essential for consumer protection, there's a risk that overly stringent regulations could stifle innovation. Future DeFi initiatives will need to find a middle ground that fosters innovation while ensuring consumer protection.

Infrastructure Vulnerabilities

- **Dependence on Technology:** The reliance on technological infrastructure exposes DeFi systems to risks such as network failures, power outages, or internet disruptions. Future developments in decentralized finance must prioritize resilience and redundancy in their infrastructure.

In conclusion, the road ahead for decentralized finance is fraught with challenges pertaining to security and privacy. From combating sophisticated cyber threats to navigating the complex web of regulatory compliance and ensuring user privacy, the DeFi landscape is in a state of continual evolution. Future advancements in this field must not only address these challenges head-on but also do so in a way that upholds the ethos of decentralization - autonomy, privacy, and security. As we forge ahead, the narrative of DeFi will be shaped by how effectively it can balance these crucial aspects, ensuring a secure, private, and resilient financial ecosystem for the digital age.

Resilience and Vulnerabilities

As we stand on the precipice of a digital currency revolution, the resilience and vulnerabilities of this burgeoning infrastructure demand our focused attention. The journey ahead is not without its obstacles, but it is paved with opportunities for innovative solutions.

Building Resilient Infrastructure

- **Robust Network Architecture:** The future of digital currency hinges on creating an infrastructure that is not only efficient but also resilient to various forms of disruptions. This includes diversifying data centers, using decentralized cloud storage solutions, and implementing fail-safe mechanisms to ensure continuous operation.

- **Case Studies of Resilience:** Consider the resilience shown by blockchain networks during high volatility periods or cyber-attacks.

These instances provide valuable lessons in designing robust digital currency systems.

Offline Transaction Capabilities

- **Bridging the Digital Divide:** One of the critical vulnerabilities of digital currency is its reliance on internet connectivity. Future innovations could focus on developing methods for offline transactions, perhaps using technologies like Bluetooth, NFC, or even QR codes, to ensure accessibility in areas with limited internet access.

- **Real-World Applications:** Projects like Bitcoin's Lightning Network, which enables fast, off-chain transactions, can be examined as a precursor to more comprehensive offline solutions.

Technological Innovations for Security

- **Quantum-Resistant Algorithms:** As quantum computing emerges, the cryptographic foundations of digital currencies face new threats. Future developments must include quantum-resistant algorithms to safeguard against these advanced computational capabilities.

- **Innovative Security Solutions:** Explore the potential of AI in detecting and preventing security breaches, the use of biometrics for enhanced user authentication, and the deployment of advanced encryption techniques for data protection.

Ensuring Systemic Stability

- **Mitigating Risks of Centralization:** While centralized digital currencies like CBDCs offer efficiency, they also concentrate risk. Future strategies could involve creating decentralized layers within these systems to distribute risk more evenly.

- **Stress Testing and Scenario Planning:** Regular stress testing and robust scenario planning will be crucial in identifying potential points of failure and addressing them proactively.

In conclusion, the path to a resilient and secure digital currency infrastructure is not straightforward. It requires a blend of technological innovation, foresight, and a commitment to continuous improvement. From developing robust network architectures to exploring offline transaction capabilities and quantum-resistant security measures, the future calls for a multifaceted approach. As we navigate these challenges, we must remain vigilant, adaptive, and innovative, ensuring that the digital currency landscape is not only efficient and accessible but also resilient and secure for generations to come.

Chapter 11
The Global Push for CBDCs: Motivations and Narratives

Introduction to the Global Stance on CBDCs

Understanding the Global Perspective

In the realm of financial evolution, Central Bank Digital Currencies (CBDCs) have emerged as a pivotal point of discussion among global entities and governments. The perspective on CBDCs ranges from enthusiastic adoption to cautious exploration. This section offers an overview of how these major players view and promote the concept of CBDCs, delving into their motivations and the narratives they craft around this digital transformation.

Diverse Global Approaches to CBDCs

- **Technological Innovation and Economic Modernization:** Many governments advocate for CBDCs as a pathway to modernize their economies. They emphasize the potential benefits of integrating advanced digital solutions into their monetary systems, such as enhancing transaction efficiency, boosting economic growth, and maintaining a competitive edge in the global financial arena.

- **Strategic Responses to Decentralized Cryptocurrencies:** As cryptocurrencies like Bitcoin gain popularity, some governments view CBDCs as a strategic tool to maintain control over financial systems and ensure monetary stability. CBDCs are seen as a way to offer a regulated, state-backed digital currency alternative, aiming to provide the benefits of digitalization while retaining state oversight.

- **Balancing Act between Innovation and Control:** Different nations have varying degrees of enthusiasm for CBDCs, influenced by their unique economic, political, and social landscapes. Countries with strong, centralized financial systems may view CBDCs as a natural evolution, while others with decentralized or fragmented systems may approach CBDCs with more caution, considering the broader implications for financial freedom and privacy.

Global Entities Shaping the CBDC Narrative

- **Influential Financial Institutions and Bodies:** Organizations like the International Monetary Fund (IMF), the World Bank, and the Bank for International Settlements (BIS) play significant roles in shaping the dialogue and policies surrounding CBDCs. These entities often provide thought leadership, research, and policy guidance, influencing how countries approach the development and implementation of CBDCs.

- **Interplay between Global Finance and CBDCs:** The adoption of CBDCs is not happening in isolation. It's intertwined with broader global financial trends, including shifts in trade, investment, and economic policy. These dynamics influence how countries perceive the risks and benefits of CBDCs and shape their approaches accordingly.

The Critical Role of Governance in CBDC Development

- **Governance and Policy Frameworks:** The development of CBDCs is deeply rooted in the governance and policy frameworks of individual nations. The way each country governs its financial system, the legal and regulatory environment, and the level of technological infrastructure all play crucial roles in shaping their stance on CBDCs.

- **Global Financial Stability Considerations:** As nations explore CBDCs, there's a growing recognition of the need to consider their impact on global financial stability. This involves understanding how CBDCs interact with existing financial systems, their potential to disrupt traditional banking, and their implications for international monetary policy.

In summary, the global stance on CBDCs is a tapestry of varied perspectives, motivations, and strategies. This intricate picture reflects the complexities of integrating groundbreaking digital currency systems into the diverse financial landscapes of the world's economies. As we navigate this new territory, understanding these global perspectives is key to grasping the potential impact of CBDCs on future financial systems.

The Role of International Organizations

Influential Organizations and Their CBDC Perspectives

The discourse around Central Bank Digital Currencies (CBDCs) is significantly influenced by major international organizations. Entities like the United Nations (UN), World Economic Forum (WEF), International Monetary Fund (IMF), and others play pivotal roles in shaping the global narrative on CBDCs. Their positions and statements carry weight, often guiding national policies and global financial strategies.

Motivations Behind the Push for CBDCs

- **Control and Surveillance:** A critical view reveals that one of the underlying motivations for these organizations' push for CBDCs is control. The digital nature of CBDCs allows for unprecedented oversight and surveillance of financial transactions, potentially leading to heightened monitoring and control over citizens' financial activities.

- **Global Financial Integration:** These organizations often promote CBDCs as tools for global financial integration. The idea is to create a more interconnected and seamless global financial system. However, this comes with its complexities, as it might lead to a consolidation of power in the hands of a few global entities, potentially diminishing the financial sovereignty of individual nations.

Propaganda and Influence on Public Perception

- **Messaging Strategies:** The communication strategies employed by these organizations are designed to portray CBDCs in a positive light. They emphasize the safety, convenience, and modernity of CBDCs, contrasting them with the often depicted risky and unstable nature of decentralized cryptocurrencies.

- **Shaping Public Opinion:** These narratives play a crucial role in shaping public opinion, swaying it towards a more accepting and favorable view of state-controlled digital currencies. However, this can sometimes overshadow the critical discussions around privacy, freedom, and the implications of such centralized control.

Critical Analysis of Organizational Motives

- **Scrutiny of Intentions:** It's important to critically analyze the intentions of these influential bodies. While their push for CBDCs is often couched in terms of economic advancement and stability, it's crucial to question whether these motivations align with the broader public interest or if they serve more to consolidate control and surveillance capabilities.

- **Global Financial Power Dynamics:** The advocacy for CBDCs by these organizations can significantly impact global financial power dynamics. It could lead to a reshaping of the global economic landscape, where the balance of financial power might shift towards entities that control and regulate digital currencies.

In summary, the role of international organizations in the push for CBDCs is a critical aspect to consider. Their influence extends beyond mere policy guidance – it shapes the global financial narrative, often blurring the lines between economic advancement and the potential for increased centralized control and surveillance. As we delve deeper into the era of digital currencies, understanding these motivations and narratives becomes crucial in navigating the future of global finance.

Propaganda and Public Perception

Crafting the CBDC Narrative

Central Bank Digital Currencies (CBDCs) are not just financial tools but also subjects of intricate messaging and communication strategies. These strategies are designed to shape public perception, creating a narrative that positions CBDCs as the safer and more convenient future of currency.

Contrasting Depictions

- **CBDCs as Safe and Convenient:** The portrayal of CBDCs often emphasizes their safety, backed by state authority and regulation. This narrative positions CBDCs as a reliable alternative to traditional banking systems, promising ease of use, enhanced security, and greater efficiency in financial transactions.

- **Decentralized Currencies as Risky:** In contrast, decentralized currencies like Bitcoin are often depicted as risky or unstable. This portrayal focuses on their volatility, the lack of regulatory oversight, and their use in illicit activities, painting a picture of uncertainty and danger.

Analysis of Messaging Strategies

- **Influencing Public Opinion:** These contrasting depictions are powerful tools in influencing public opinion towards the adoption of CBDCs. By highlighting the benefits of CBDCs and the risks of decentralized currencies, governing bodies and financial institutions can sway public sentiment in favor of state-controlled digital currencies.

- **Underlying Motivations:** However, these messaging strategies may have underlying motivations. They serve not just to inform but also to align public opinion with governmental and institutional agendas, which may prioritize control and surveillance over financial autonomy and privacy.

Addressing the Imbalance

- **Critical Reception:** It's essential to critically assess the information being presented. While CBDCs offer certain advantages, the negative portrayal of decentralized currencies often neglects their benefits, such as financial autonomy, privacy, and freedom from centralized control.

- **Balanced Discourse:** Encouraging a more balanced discourse that acknowledges the pros and cons of both CBDCs and decentralized currencies is vital. This would ensure a more informed public, capable of understanding and engaging with the future of digital currencies from a place of knowledge rather than fear or misinformation.

In summary, the narrative around CBDCs and decentralized currencies is shaped significantly by contrasting portrayals. While CBDCs are often presented as safe and user-friendly, decentralized currencies are frequently depicted as risky. This imbalance in messaging influences public perception, underlining the need for a more nuanced and balanced discussion about the future of digital currencies.

Control vs. Freedom in Digital Currency

The Narrative of Control

- **Financial Surveillance:** Central Bank Digital Currencies (CBDCs) present a potential tool for governments to exercise unprecedented levels of financial surveillance. With CBDCs, every transaction could be traceable, giving governments the ability to monitor and analyze spending patterns in real time.

- **Control Over Financial Activities:** Beyond surveillance, CBDCs could allow governments to exert control over citizens' financial activities. This might include the ability to freeze assets, control spending, and even exclude certain individuals or groups from the financial system based on their activities or political stance.

- **Policy Implementation:** Governments could use CBDCs to implement and enforce economic policies directly. For instance, CBDCs could be programmed for specific uses, like ensuring welfare funds are spent on essentials, thereby exerting a form of control over personal spending.

The Promise of Freedom

- **Decentralized Currencies as a Counterbalance:** In contrast, decentralized currencies like Bitcoin represent a form of financial freedom and autonomy. They operate independently of centralized authorities, giving users control over their assets without government intervention.

- **Privacy and Anonymity:** Decentralized currencies offer greater levels of privacy. Transactions can be conducted without the need for personal identification, safeguarding users' anonymity and protecting them from potential surveillance.

- **Autonomy in Financial Decisions:** With decentralized currencies, individuals have the autonomy to make financial decisions without fear of government oversight or intervention. This freedom extends to cross-border transactions, which can be conducted without the need for state approval or currency controls.

Balancing Control and Freedom

- **The Need for a Balanced Approach:** The contrasting narratives of control (CBDCs) and freedom (decentralized currencies) highlight a need for balance. While governments seek to maintain financial order and security, the autonomy and privacy of individuals must also be respected.

- **Potential for Coexistence:** The future might see a coexistence of CBDCs and decentralized currencies, each serving different needs and preferences. CBDCs could be used for everyday transactions within a regulated framework, while decentralized currencies could be used where privacy and autonomy are priorities.

In conclusion, the debate between CBDCs and decentralized currencies is fundamentally a debate between control and freedom. While CBDCs offer advantages in terms of efficiency and security, they also raise concerns about surveillance and control. On the other hand, decentralized currencies promise privacy and autonomy but come with their own set of challenges. A nuanced understanding of these dynamics is crucial as we navigate the evolving landscape of digital currencies.

Case Studies and Global Examples

As countries around the globe navigate the complexities of introducing Central Bank Digital Currencies (CBDCs), a range of case studies emerge, each offering unique insights into the aspirations, challenges, and public reactions surrounding these initiatives.

- **China's Digital Yuan (e-CNY):** China stands as a frontrunner in the CBDC landscape with its Digital Yuan initiative. Spearheaded by the People's Bank of China, the e-CNY aims to digitize a portion of China's currency, enhancing transaction efficiency and strengthening government oversight. While the initiative is marked by technological advancement and potential internationalization of the Yuan, it also raises public concerns regarding privacy and state surveillance.

- **The Bahamas' Sand Dollar:** In the Bahamas, the introduction of the Sand Dollar aims to foster financial inclusion across its archipelago. The digital currency addresses the challenges of maintaining traditional banking infrastructure across numerous islands, offering a digital alternative accessible to all citizens. This initiative is particularly notable for small economies or regions with geographical challenges, providing a blueprint for digital currency implementation.

- **Sweden's E-Krona Project:** Sweden's declining cash usage has led to the exploration of the e-Krona. This project is still in its testing phase, with a focus on understanding the coexistence of a digital currency alongside traditional cash. It has sparked a national debate on digital literacy, privacy, and the future role of cash in Sweden's economy.

- **India's Digital Rupee:** The Reserve Bank of India's exploration of a digital rupee seeks to enhance financial inclusion and reduce cash management costs. Given India's vast and diverse population, the project faces challenges around technological access and varying financial literacy levels. The successful implementation of a digital rupee could revolutionize the financial landscape in one of the world's largest economies.

The public responses to CBDCs vary significantly across these case studies. Privacy concerns are a common thread, as citizens grapple with the potential for increased government surveillance. Technological challenges, such as access to necessary infrastructure and varying levels of digital literacy, also play a crucial role in public acceptance. Furthermore, the economic impacts and cultural acceptance of CBDCs differ, reflecting the diverse global perspectives on digital currency adoption.

As more countries venture into the realm of digital currencies, these examples continue to inform and shape our understanding of their potential impact on global finance. The ongoing narrative of CBDCs is a complex one, intertwining technological innovation with societal and economic implications.

In summary, the exploration of CBDCs across various countries presents a tapestry of motivations, challenges, and public reactions. These case studies provide valuable insights into the potential paths CBDCs could take and their impacts on societies and economies worldwide. As more countries experiment with and launch their digital currencies, these examples will continue to shape our understanding of the future of global finance.

Future Implications

The ascent of Central Bank Digital Currencies (CBDCs) heralds a transformative era in global finance. Their widespread adoption could fundamentally alter not just the mechanics of money, but also the underlying dynamics of economic power, individual financial freedom, and global economic relationships.

- **A World Dominated by CBDCs:** In a scenario where CBDCs become the norm, we'd see a radical shift in how money is controlled and distributed. Governments and central banks would gain unprecedented control over the financial system. Every transaction could potentially be monitored, and financial policies could be implemented with striking precision. While this might enhance economic policy effectiveness, it also raises concerns about state overreach and the erosion of financial privacy.

- **Shift in Global Economic Power:** The adoption of CBDCs could also redefine the global economic pecking order. Nations with advanced digital currency systems might exert greater influence in international trade and finance. The dynamics of currency reserves and international lending could shift, favoring countries with robust digital financial infrastructures. Moreover, the role of traditional global currencies like the U.S. dollar could be challenged, potentially leading to a more multipolar currency world.

- **The Balance of Financial Freedom:** One of the most critical implications of a CBDC-dominant world is its impact on individual financial freedom. The ability of governments to track and potentially control spending could lead to a scenario where financial autonomy is compromised. The concept of money as a means of anonymous exchange might become obsolete, replaced by a system where every cent is accounted for and controlled.

- **Contrasting Decentralized Alternatives:** In this landscape, decentralized currencies could either flourish as a counterbalance, offering a haven for those seeking financial autonomy, or they could be marginalized, pushed to the fringes by powerful, state-backed digital currencies. The competition between centralized and decentralized currencies could define the future of money, each representing divergent philosophies of freedom and control.

- **Global Economic Dynamics:** The adoption of CBDCs will likely impact global economic stability and the nature of economic crises. The ability of central banks to implement monetary policies directly through CBDCs could lead to more effective responses to financial crises. However, it could also lead to new types of economic vulnerabilities, particularly if digital currencies become a target for cyberattacks or if technical failures occur in these systems.

As we stand at the cusp of this potential shift, it's crucial to ponder the long-term consequences. Will the convenience and efficiency of CBDCs outweigh the concerns over privacy and autonomy? How will the world navigate the new challenges posed by this digital financial revolution? The answers to these questions will shape not just our wallets, but our world in the decades to come.

The Advocacy for Decentralized Alternatives

In the evolving narrative of digital currencies, the advocacy for decentralized alternatives stands as a significant counterpoint to the rise of Central Bank Digital Currencies (CBDCs). This movement, grounded in a blend of technological innovation, economic theory, and a quest for financial autonomy, presents a compelling case for the continued relevance and importance of decentralized currencies like Bitcoin and Ethereum.

- **The Case for Decentralization:** Advocates for decentralized currencies argue that these digital assets offer a level of financial freedom and privacy unattainable with CBDCs. Unlike state-controlled digital currencies, decentralized currencies operate on a peer-to-peer network, free from direct government oversight and control. This structure is seen as a bastion against potential financial censorship and surveillance, ensuring that individuals retain autonomy over their financial transactions. Moreover, decentralized currencies are lauded for their potential to create a more inclusive financial system, reaching individuals and communities underserved by traditional banking.

- **Balancing Control with Freedom:** The conversation around decentralized currencies is not just a technical or economic one; it's deeply rooted in philosophical beliefs about the role of money in society and the balance between state control and individual freedom. Advocates emphasize the importance of having alternatives to state-run currencies, particularly in scenarios where government policies might infringe on personal liberties or where economic mismanagement leads to financial instability.

- **Educational Initiatives and Public Discourse:** A key aspect of this advocacy is education. Through public forums, online platforms, and educational initiatives, proponents of decentralized finance work to demystify blockchain technology and cryptocurrencies. They aim to inform the public about the benefits and risks of both decentralized and centralized digital currencies, fostering a more informed and engaged citizenry.

- **Grassroots Movements and Community Engagement:** The decentralized currency movement is also characterized by robust grassroots involvement. From online communities to local meetups, these groups provide platforms for discussion, innovation, and collaboration. They play a critical role in shaping the development and adoption of decentralized technologies, often serving as testing grounds for new ideas and applications.

- **Shaping the Future of Digital Currencies:** As the debate over the future of money continues, the role of these advocacy groups becomes increasingly vital. They not only provide a counterbalance to the narrative pushed by proponents of CBDCs but also ensure that the evolution of digital currencies remains diverse, dynamic, and aligned with the broader needs and values of society.

In summary, the advocacy for decentralized alternatives to CBDCs is a multifaceted endeavor, combining technological innovation with a strong commitment to financial autonomy and privacy. As the world grapples with the implications of digital currencies, the voices of these advocates will be crucial in ensuring a balanced, equitable, and inclusive financial future.

Conclusion: The Path Forward

As we conclude our exploration into the rapidly evolving landscape of digital currencies, it's essential to pause and reflect on the path ahead. The journey into the world of Central Bank Digital Currencies (CBDCs) and decentralized alternatives is not just a financial or technological endeavor; it's a journey that touches upon the very fabric of global economics, individual freedom, and societal values.

The Crucial Role of Informed Decision-Making: The future of digital currencies will be significantly shaped by the decisions made today by policymakers, technologists, and, crucially, everyday citizens. Informed decision-making, therefore, becomes paramount. It's essential that all stakeholders – from the most tech-savvy to the average consumer – are equipped with a clear understanding of both CBDCs and decentralized alternatives. This understanding should encompass not just the operational aspects but the broader economic, social, and ethical implications of these digital currencies.

Fostering Public Discourse: Public discourse is vital in shaping the future of digital currencies. Open, transparent, and inclusive conversations that bring together diverse viewpoints can pave the way for more democratic and fair financial systems. These discussions should transcend national boundaries, reflecting the global nature of finance and technology. They should also be inclusive, ensuring that voices from different economic backgrounds, cultures, and levels of technological expertise are heard and considered.

The Balance Between Innovation and Ethics: As we move forward, balancing technological innovation with ethical considerations will be crucial. The allure of technological advancements should not overshadow the need for privacy, security, and equity. The development of digital currencies should be aligned with the broader goals of societal welfare and global economic stability.

Embracing a Multifaceted Approach: The future of money will likely not be a binary choice between CBDCs and decentralized currencies. Instead, a more nuanced and multifaceted financial ecosystem might emerge, one that harnesses the strengths of both systems while mitigating their weaknesses. This future will require collaboration and dialogue among various sectors – finance, technology, government, and civil society.

A Call for Ethical Stewardship: Ultimately, the journey ahead calls for ethical stewardship. It requires a commitment to not only advance the frontiers of technology and finance but to do so in a manner that serves humanity's best interests. It calls for a future where digital currencies empower rather than alienate, include rather than exclude, and bring transparency and efficiency without sacrificing privacy and autonomy.

In concluding, "The Future of Money - The Changing Face of Global Currency" invites readers to be active participants in this journey. The future of digital currencies is not just a story to be written by the few but a narrative to be shaped by the many. It's a future that holds immense possibilities, challenges, and opportunities – a future that awaits our collective wisdom and action.

Chapter 12
The GlobeTrotter Ecosystem - Blueprint for the Ideal Digital Currency

Introduction to The GlobeTrotter Ecosystem

In the realm of financial evolution, the GlobeTrotter Ecosystem emerges as a visionary model, reshaping our understanding of currency and economic structures. This ecosystem isn't just a new currency or a financial tool; it represents a paradigm shift in how we perceive and interact with money, governance, and societal structures. The concept transcends traditional financial boundaries, introducing a world where equality, efficiency, and sustainability are not just ideals but practical realities.

At the heart of the GlobeTrotter Ecosystem is the desire to rectify inherent flaws in our current economic systems - issues like inequality, corruption, and the inefficiencies of government-run monetary systems. These problems aren't just numbers on a balance sheet; they affect real lives, widening the gap between the haves and have-nots, and often leaving the latter in a state of perpetual struggle.

Enter the GlobeTrotter Ecosystem, a holistic solution encompassing a new global economic and monetary system designed to tackle these challenges head-on. Its foundation lies in Universal Basic Income and Jobs (UBIJ), a concept that promises to eradicate poverty, bridge inequality gaps, and provide a guaranteed income to every adult and young adult in the world, independent of government control or personal circumstances.

The innovation doesn't stop there. The GlobeTrotter Ecosystem introduces a new global currency – the GlobeTrotter Globie GTC coin. This isn't just another cryptocurrency; it's a symbol of a decentralized and democratic financial system. The Globie is designed to run on a hybrid blockchain, ensuring top-tier security and speed without the excessive power consumption typical of traditional blockchain systems. This makes the currency not only secure and efficient but also environmentally conscious.

The UBIJ system, integral to the GlobeTrotter Ecosystem, is a beacon of hope and progress. It aims to level the playing field for all, removing the power from the elite and redistributing it equitably. Once a person reaches the age of 15, they automatically start receiving UBIJ, ensuring that no one falls through the cracks due to bureaucratic red tape or governmental inefficiency. This system encourages governments to prioritize the happiness and well-being of their residents, fostering a global community where each individual's success contributes to the collective prosperity.

The creation of the GlobeTrotter Ecosystem is more than an economic revolution; it's a reimagining of societal norms and values. It's about building a world where financial stability is a given, not a privilege, where governments serve the people instead of controlling them, and where each individual has the freedom and resources to pursue their aspirations. In this new world, the concept of "struggling to make ends meet" becomes a relic of the past, replaced by an environment where everyone has the opportunity to thrive.

As we delve deeper into the specifics of the GlobeTrotter Ecosystem in the subsequent sections, we'll explore how this visionary system could reshape our world, offering a glimpse into a future where economic freedom and equality are not just dreams but everyday realities.

The GlobeTrotter Currency: Concept and Design

This section delves deep into the concept and design of the GlobeTrotter Globie GTC coin and its accompanying specialty tokens, highlighting their unique features and the revolutionary hybrid blockchain technology that powers them.

- **GlobeTrotter Globie GTC Coin and Specialty Tokens:** At the core of the GlobeTrotter Ecosystem lies the GlobeTrotter Globie GTC coin, a cryptocurrency designed to redefine the global economic landscape. The GTC coin isn't just a medium of exchange; it's a symbol of financial democracy and sustainability. Alongside the Globie, the ecosystem introduces various specialty tokens, each serving specific functions, from property ownership (GTP tokens) to voting (GTV tokens) and even gift or coupon tokens (GGT tokens). These tokens represent a broad spectrum of utilities, transcending traditional financial instruments by embedding versatile functionalities directly into the currency system.

  The design of these tokens is carefully crafted to ensure broad accessibility, ease of use, and integration into everyday life. Imagine a world where your currency not only enables purchases but also empowers you to participate directly in democratic processes, own and transfer property securely, and receive rewards that align with your lifestyle and choices.

- **Hybrid Blockchain Technology: Structure and Benefits:** The GlobeTrotter Currency harnesses the power of hybrid blockchain technology, a groundbreaking innovation in the field of digital ledger technology. This system combines the best of both worlds: the decentralization and security of blockchain with the efficiency and scalability of centralized systems.

  The hybrid blockchain consists of two layers: an outer blockchain that acts as a protective shield and an inner blockchain that handles the core transactions and functionalities. This dual-layer structure offers several advantages:

  - Enhanced Security: The outer layer provides an additional security barrier, safeguarding the inner blockchain from potential attacks or vulnerabilities.

- Improved Scalability: By distributing functions across two layers, the system can handle a larger volume of transactions more efficiently, reducing bottlenecks and ensuring faster processing times.

- Flexibility: This structure allows for a customizable approach, where certain parts of the transactions can be made public for transparency, while others can remain private, maintaining confidentiality where needed.

- **Security Features: Ensuring Tamper-Proof and Secure Transactions:** Security is paramount in the GlobeTrotter Currency system. The hybrid blockchain architecture plays a crucial role in this, providing a robust framework that is virtually impervious to tampering and unauthorized access.

  - Immutable Transaction Records: Once a transaction is recorded on the blockchain, it cannot be altered or deleted, ensuring the integrity and reliability of the transaction history.

  - Cryptographic Security: Advanced cryptographic techniques are employed to secure data, making it nearly impossible for unauthorized parties to decipher or manipulate the information.

  - Decentralized Consensus: The system utilizes a decentralized consensus mechanism, eliminating single points of failure and reducing the risk of manipulation or control by any one entity.

In conclusion, the GlobeTrotter Currency, with its innovative Globie GTC coin and specialty tokens, powered by a pioneering hybrid blockchain technology, stands as a testament to the potential of digital currencies to revolutionize the global economy. This section not only elucidates the technical intricacies of this system but also paints a vivid picture of its potential to democratize finance, ensuring security, efficiency, and transparency for all users. As we delve further into the GlobeTrotter Ecosystem, we uncover how this currency is poised to be more than just a financial tool – it's a catalyst for a more equitable and empowered global society.

Universal Basic Income and Jobs (UBIJ)

This revolutionary concept represents a radical shift in addressing economic disparities, altering the landscape of poverty, inequality, and the job market.

- **Concept and Implementation of UBIJ in the GlobeTrotter Ecosystem:** The UBIJ model is a transformative approach that guarantees a basic income for every adult and young adult worldwide, regardless of their employment status. It is a completely self-financing system. This system, a cornerstone of the GlobeTrotter Ecosystem, is ingeniously designed to ensure financial stability and dignity for all individuals. The implementation of UBIJ involves distributing a predetermined amount of GlobeTrotter Globie GTC coins monthly to every eligible individual. This distribution is automated and executed through the GlobeTrotter Ecosystem's hybrid blockchain technology, ensuring efficiency, transparency, and security.

  The design of the UBIJ system addresses the challenges arising from automation and AI in the job market. As these technologies evolve, traditional job roles may diminish, making the UBIJ not just a social safety net but a necessary adaptation to the changing economic environment. Moreover, the UBIJ system is designed to create job opportunities for those who wish to work, encompassing various sectors and industries, thus fostering a dynamic and inclusive job market.

- **Impact on Poverty, Inequality, and Job Market Dynamics:** The introduction of UBIJ is poised to have profound implications on global socio-economic structures:

- Eradication of Extreme Poverty: UBIJ provides a financial floor for everyone, ensuring basic needs such as food, shelter, and healthcare are met. This is a direct approach to eradicating extreme poverty.

- Reduction of Inequality: By providing everyone with a basic income, the wealth gap narrows significantly. It empowers people to pursue education, entrepreneurial ventures, or creative endeavors, leveling the playing field across socio-economic strata.

- Transformation of the Job Market: With basic needs met, individuals can choose jobs based on interest and aptitude rather than sheer necessity. This could lead to a more satisfied and productive workforce, and a surge in innovation and creativity in various sectors.

- **Mechanisms for Distribution and Eligibility Criteria**: The distribution mechanism of UBIJ is underpinned by the advanced hybrid blockchain technology of the GlobeTrotter Ecosystem. This technology ensures a seamless, transparent, and tamper-proof disbursement of the basic income. Each individual in the system is identified through a unique, secure digital ID, ensuring that the income reaches the rightful recipient.

Eligibility for UBIJ is straightforward and inclusive:

- Age Criteria: All adults, defined as individuals aged 15 and above, are eligible to receive the full UBIJ amount. Young adults, typically between the ages of 13 and 17, receive a reduced amount, recognizing their transition towards adulthood.

- Global Inclusivity: There are no geographical boundaries for eligibility. Every individual, irrespective of their country of residence, is entitled to receive UBIJ, promoting global economic inclusivity.

- No Employment Conditions: Unlike traditional welfare systems, receiving UBIJ is not contingent on employment status, making it a true universal basic income.

In conclusion, the UBIJ model within the GlobeTrotter Ecosystem represents a bold and hopeful vision for the future of global economics. It promises not just a financial safety net, but a foundation upon which individuals can build a life of choice and opportunity, free from the constraints of economic hardship.

Empowering Individuals through Financial Independence and Equity

This section delves into the revolutionary ways GlobeTrotter reshapes the economic landscape, offering a more equitable and inclusive financial future for all.

- **Promoting Financial Independence for Every Individual:** The GlobeTrotter Ecosystem fundamentally transforms the concept of financial independence, making it a tangible reality for every individual. At the heart of this transformation is the Universal Basic Income and Jobs (UBIJ) model. The UBIJ initiative ensures a steady, unconditional flow of income to all adults, courtesy of the GlobeTrotter Globie GTC coin. This financial stability is not just about meeting basic needs; it's about empowering people to make independent life choices. Whether it's pursuing education, starting a business, or exploring creative avenues, the financial support from UBIJ acts as a catalyst for individuals to chase their dreams without the constant worry of financial survival. This paradigm shift not only nurtures a society of more fulfilled individuals but also sparks innovation and drives progress in various fields.

- **Eliminating the Unemployment Trap and Reducing Government Bureaucracy:** One of the most significant impacts of the GlobeTrotter Ecosystem is its ability to eliminate the 'unemployment trap'. In traditional systems, individuals receiving welfare benefits often face a dilemma: earning too much can result in a loss of benefits, sometimes leaving them financially worse off than before. GlobeTrotter's UBIJ model eradicates this trap. As individuals earn more, they don't lose their basic income; instead, it supplements their earnings, encouraging employment and entrepreneurship.

Moreover, the GlobeTrotter Ecosystem significantly trims government bureaucracy. The administration of welfare programs often involves complex eligibility criteria, extensive paperwork, and substantial administrative overhead. By replacing these programs with a universal basic income, the need for such bureaucracies is vastly reduced, leading to more efficient use of resources and reducing the burden on taxpayers.

- **Addressing the Gender Pay Gap and Increasing Bargaining Power for Workers:** The GlobeTrotter Ecosystem also takes strides in addressing the persistent issue of the gender pay gap. By ensuring that every adult, regardless of gender, receives a basic income, women are afforded a level of financial security and independence. This empowerment is particularly crucial for women in lower-income brackets or those in precarious employment situations. The gender pay gap narrows as the basic income provides a solid financial foundation for all, making women less dependent on employment income and more resilient to economic fluctuations.

Furthermore, the UBIJ model dramatically increases the bargaining power of workers. With the assurance of a basic income, employees are no longer forced to accept unfavorable job conditions out of financial necessity. This shift rebalances the power dynamics between employers and employees, compelling businesses to offer better wages, benefits, and working conditions to attract and retain talent. It also diminishes the need for extensive labor market regulations, such as minimum wage laws, as the market naturally adjusts to these new economic realities.

In summary, the GlobeTrotter Ecosystem is not just a financial model; it's a blueprint for societal transformation. It fosters a world where financial independence and equity are not mere aspirations but everyday realities. By eliminating the unemployment trap, reducing government bureaucracy, addressing the gender pay gap, and increasing the bargaining power of workers, GlobeTrotter paves the way for a more equitable, just, and prosperous global society. This chapter not only elucidates the mechanisms of this transformation but also invites readers to envision a future where economic barriers are dismantled, and every individual is empowered to realize their full potential.

The Smart Wallet: Simplifying Transactions and Contracts

Here, we delve into the innovative Smart Wallet, a cornerstone of the GlobeTrotter Ecosystem. This section unpacks the sophisticated yet user-friendly features of the GlobeTrotter smart wallet, its role in facilitating simple smart contracts, and its integrated voting system, all of which significantly influence both personal and business financial management.

- **Features of the GlobeTrotter Smart Wallet:** The GlobeTrotter smart wallet represents a leap forward in digital currency management. It's designed to be more than just a wallet; it's a comprehensive financial management tool. One of its standout features is its intuitive user interface, which simplifies the complexity often associated with digital currencies. Users can easily track their transactions, manage their GlobeTrotter Globie GTC coins and specialty tokens, and access a detailed history of their financial activities.

  Moreover, the wallet integrates advanced security protocols, ensuring the safety and privacy of transactions. Utilizing biometric verification methods such as fingerprint scanning and facial recognition, the wallet offers users peace of mind, knowing their assets are protected against unauthorized access. This security is coupled with real-time synchronization with the GlobeTrotter blockchain, guaranteeing that users' financial data is continuously updated and accurate.

- **Creation of Simple Smart Contracts and a Built-in Voting System:** A remarkable innovation within the GlobeTrotter smart wallet is its ability to create and manage smart contracts. These contracts are not only secure and legally binding but also user-friendly. Users can customize their contracts by selecting from a range of predefined conditions, making the process accessible even for those without a technical background. This feature democratizes the use of smart contracts, opening up numerous possibilities for personal and business applications.

Additionally, the wallet features a built-in voting system, a key element in the decentralized decision-making process of the GlobeTrotter Ecosystem. Users can participate in community votes, have their say in key ecosystem decisions, and contribute to the democratic governance of the system. This function empowers users to be active stakeholders in the ecosystem, fostering a sense of community and shared responsibility.

- **Impact on Personal and Business Financial Management:** The GlobeTrotter smart wallet has a transformative impact on personal and business financial management. For individuals, it simplifies the management of digital assets, making it easier to track spending, savings, and investments. The ability to create smart contracts for personal agreements, such as loans or payments, adds a layer of security and convenience to personal finance.

For businesses, the wallet streamlines financial operations. Companies can manage their transactions with ease, create smart contracts for business deals, and ensure compliance with regulatory requirements through the immutable record-keeping of the blockchain. The voting feature also allows businesses to participate in ecosystem governance, influencing decisions that may impact their operations.

In essence, the GlobeTrotter smart wallet is not just a tool for financial transactions; it's an all-encompassing platform that enhances the user's control over their financial life. It embodies the ethos of the GlobeTrotter Ecosystem - empowerment, security, and simplicity - and serves as a bridge to a future where managing digital currency is as straightforward and secure as using traditional money.

In conclusion, the GlobeTrotter smart wallet is a pivotal component of the GlobeTrotter Ecosystem, revolutionizing how we think about and interact with digital currencies. Its impact extends far beyond mere financial transactions; it reshapes the landscape of personal and business financial management, bringing the power of blockchain technology to the fingertips of its users. This chapter not only provides an in-depth exploration of the wallet's features and capabilities but also invites readers to envision a future where financial management is seamlessly integrated into our daily lives, empowered by the innovative GlobeTrotter Ecosystem.

Decentralization: Power to the People

In this section, we explore the core principle that underpins the GlobeTrotter Ecosystem: Decentralization. This section elaborates on the mechanisms that ensure the decentralization of this digital currency, detailing its independence from governmental control, the participatory role of the general population in its governance, and the checks and balances designed to prevent any potential abuse by elites.

- **Mechanisms Ensuring Decentralization and Independence from Governments:** The GlobeTrotter Ecosystem is built on a foundational commitment to decentralization, ensuring that it operates independently of any central governmental authority. This is achieved through the use of advanced hybrid blockchain technology, which provides a secure, transparent, and tamper-proof platform for financial transactions and voting. Unlike traditional financial systems, where central banks and governments exert considerable control, the GlobeTrotter Ecosystem is managed collectively by its users.

A key feature of this ecosystem is its two-layered blockchain structure. The outer blockchain layer serves as a protective shield, safeguarding the inner layer where transactions occur. This design not only enhances security but also fortifies the system against external influences, including potential governmental interference. The hybrid nature of the blockchain combines the best attributes of both public and private blockchains, providing the transparency and security of public blockchains with the speed and efficiency of private ones.

- **Role of the General Population in Managing and Voting on Ecosystem Matters:** In the GlobeTrotter Ecosystem, the general population plays a critical role in managing and making decisions. Each member of the ecosystem has an equal voice and vote in significant matters, facilitated by the integrated voting system within the smart wallet. This democratization of financial governance empowers every user to contribute to the direction and policies of the ecosystem.

Voting on ecosystem matters is not just a privilege but a responsibility for every user. Decisions on everything from updates to the blockchain protocol to new feature implementations are put to a vote, ensuring that changes in the ecosystem reflect the collective will of its users. This participatory approach fosters a sense of ownership and engagement among users, as they are directly involved in shaping the ecosystem's future.

- **Checks and Balances: Keeping Elites and Potential Abuse in Check:** To prevent the concentration of power and influence among a select few, the GlobeTrotter Ecosystem incorporates robust checks and balances. These measures are designed to deter potential abuses of power by elites or any other group seeking to manipulate the system for personal gain.

One such measure is the transparent and immutable recording of all transactions and votes on the blockchain. This level of transparency ensures that any attempt to exert undue influence or engage in corrupt practices is visible to all users, promoting accountability and ethical conduct. Furthermore, the voting system is designed to be resistant to manipulation, with safeguards in place to prevent vote-rigging or coercion.

Additionally, the GlobeTrotter Ecosystem implements algorithmic regulations that automatically detect and flag any anomalous activities suggestive of power consolidation or abuse. These regulations are constantly reviewed and updated through community consensus, adapting to new challenges and threats to the decentralized nature of the ecosystem.

In conclusion, the GlobeTrotter Ecosystem embodies a paradigm shift in the way financial systems operate. By prioritizing decentralization, empowering the general population, and instituting strong checks and balances, it offers a blueprint for a financial system that is not only technologically advanced but also inherently democratic and fair. This chapter provides a comprehensive exploration of these principles, inviting readers to envision a future where financial power truly belongs to the people, and where the potential for abuse by elites is effectively curtailed.

Physical Cash and Global Transactions

We will delve into the intriguing domain of the GlobeTrotter Ecosystem, specifically focusing on the integration of physical cash and the handling of global transactions in a world where digital currency reigns supreme. This section addresses the unique challenges and innovative solutions associated with maintaining a robust and resilient financial ecosystem, particularly in scenarios where traditional digital connectivity might be compromised.

- **The Need for Physical Currency in the GlobeTrotter Ecosystem:** In the GlobeTrotter Ecosystem, a revolutionary approach is adopted, eliminating the need for traditional physical currency. Instead, the ecosystem is fully digital, with a unique functionality that ensures seamless transactions even during internet or power grid shutdowns. This is achieved through the innovative use of smartphones as the primary medium for financial exchanges.

In the GlobeTrotter Ecosystem, each smartphone acts as a secure wallet, storing the user's financial balance and enabling offline transactions. When the device is offline, transactions are recorded locally and then synchronized with the blockchain once the connection is restored. This method ensures continuous functionality and access to funds, regardless of external connectivity issues.

This approach effectively negates the necessity for physical tokens or cash, as the system maintains its integrity and operability even in scenarios where traditional digital systems might fail. The resilience of this method lies in its decentralization and the use of cutting-edge technology, ensuring that each user's assets are protected and accessible at all times. The GlobeTrotter Ecosystem thus offers a futuristic and robust solution, where the concept of physical currency is replaced by a reliable and secure digital alternative, providing users with unprecedented financial freedom and security.

- **Functionality During Internet or Power Grid Shutdowns:** One of the most innovative aspects of the GlobeTrotter Ecosystem is its ability to operate seamlessly, even in the absence of internet connectivity or during power outages. This is achieved through the unique design of the GlobeTrotter smart wallet, which stores the real balance on the smartphone itself. The blockchain serves as a backup, recording all transactions.

In the event of a network or power failure, users can still access their balances and make transactions using their smart wallets. Once connectivity is restored, these transactions are synchronized with the blockchain, ensuring that all records are up-to-date and consistent. This offline functionality is a crucial aspect of the GlobeTrotter Ecosystem, ensuring uninterrupted financial operations regardless of external conditions.

- **Handling Global Transactions: Efficiency and Scalability:** The GlobeTrotter Ecosystem is designed to handle global transactions with unparalleled efficiency and scalability. Leveraging blockchain technology and AI, it streamlines international money transfers, making them faster, more secure, and free, being less costly compared to traditional banking systems.

In the GlobeTrotter Ecosystem, the concept of "international transactions" is transformed, as it operates as the sole financial system globally, thus eliminating the need for currency conversions. This unified approach simplifies financial exchanges across borders, doing away with the complexities and additional costs typically associated with currency exchange. The advanced technological infrastructure of the Ecosystem is designed for scalability, adeptly managing millions of transactions simultaneously. This capability ensures that transactions are processed swiftly and securely, regardless of their global origin or destination. This system's seamless and unified nature represents a significant leap forward in global financial transactions, offering efficiency and reliability on an unprecedented scale.

The decentralized nature of the GlobeTrotter Ecosystem also means that it is not limited by national borders or traditional banking regulations. This global reach empowers users from all corners of the world to engage in financial transactions with ease and confidence.

In summary, the GlobeTrotter Ecosystem's approach to integrating physical cash and handling global transactions is a testament to its commitment to security, resilience, and user convenience. This chapter paints a vivid picture of a financial system that is not only technologically advanced but also adaptable and robust, capable of withstanding and operating effectively under a variety of conditions. It invites readers to imagine a future where financial transactions are seamless, secure, and accessible to all, regardless of geographical boundaries or unforeseen disruptions.

Environmental and Social Responsibility

In the transformative landscape of digital currency, the GlobeTrotter Ecosystem emerges as a paradigm of environmental and social responsibility, embodying the principles of sustainable and equitable development. This section delves into the minimal environmental impact and the promotion of social responsibility integral to the GlobeTrotter Ecosystem, illustrating its role as a vanguard in the realm of digital finance.

- **Minimal Environmental Impact:** The GlobeTrotter Ecosystem, at its core, is underpinned by a hybrid blockchain technology specifically engineered to minimize environmental impact. Unlike traditional cryptocurrency systems that rely on energy-intensive processes like proof-of-work, the GlobeTrotter Ecosystem employs a more energy-efficient consensus mechanism. This mechanism significantly reduces the carbon footprint associated with digital currency transactions.

  - **Low-Power Consumption**: The hybrid blockchain architecture of the GlobeTrotter Ecosystem is designed to operate with minimal energy consumption. By eliminating the need for massive computational power to validate transactions, the system drastically cuts down on electricity usage, contributing to a greener and more sustainable digital environment.

- **Renewable Energy Sources**: The infrastructure supporting the GlobeTrotter Ecosystem is predominantly powered by renewable energy sources. This commitment to green energy not only enhances the ecosystem's sustainability but also sets a new standard for digital currency platforms in terms of environmental stewardship.

- **Eco-Friendly Operations**: The GlobeTrotter Ecosystem embodies a holistic approach to environmental consciousness. From its server farms to its operational protocols, every aspect of the ecosystem is scrutinized and optimized for eco-efficiency, ensuring that the digital currency realm is in harmony with ecological preservation.

- **Promoting Social Responsibility and Equitable Development:** The GlobeTrotter Ecosystem is more than a financial platform; it's a beacon of social empowerment and equitable growth. It is engineered to foster a more inclusive and fair economic landscape, where every individual has equal opportunities to thrive.

- **Universal Basic Income (UBIJ)**: At the heart of the GlobeTrotter Ecosystem is the UBIJ, a revolutionary concept that ensures a steady income for all, irrevocably transforming the social fabric. This income guarantees basic human needs are met, diminishing the chasm of inequality and fueling a more balanced economic development.

- **Decentralization and Democracy**: The ecosystem's decentralized nature democratizes financial control, transferring power from the traditional financial elites to the individual users. This shift not only empowers individuals but also fosters a culture of collective decision-making and shared responsibility.

- **Education and Awareness**: The GlobeTrotter Ecosystem places a strong emphasis on educating its users about financial literacy, sustainable practices, and the importance of social responsibility.

This educational component is pivotal in cultivating a well-informed user base, poised to make decisions that benefit both themselves and the broader community.

- **Community Development Projects**: A portion of the ecosystem's revenue is earmarked for community development projects. These projects range from building sustainable infrastructure to funding educational and healthcare initiatives in underprivileged areas, demonstrating the ecosystem's commitment to social upliftment.

- **Ethical Investment Opportunities**: The platform offers users opportunities to invest in socially responsible and ethical ventures. These investments are not only financially rewarding but also contribute to positive social and environmental change.

In conclusion, the GlobeTrotter Ecosystem stands as a testament to the possibility of a digital currency platform that is not only environmentally conscious but also deeply committed to social responsibility and equitable development. It paves the way for a future where digital finance is seamlessly integrated with sustainable and altruistic practices, heralding a new era of conscientious currency.

Challenges, Criticisms, and Responses

The GlobeTrotter Ecosystem, a bold and visionary digital currency platform, doesn't just introduce a new financial paradigm; it reshapes the entire landscape of global economics. However, with such innovation comes inevitable challenges and criticisms. In this section, we'll delve into these potential hurdles, their implications, and the robust strategies in place to address and mitigate them, ensuring the system's resilience and future-proofing.

Addressing Potential Challenges and Criticisms

- **Security Concerns:**

  - *Criticism*: With the concentration of financial activities on digital platforms, security concerns are paramount. Critics often point out the risks of cyber attacks, data breaches, and system failures.

  - *Response*: The GlobeTrotter Ecosystem employs a multifaceted security approach, including advanced encryption, continuous system monitoring, and AI-driven threat detection. Regular security audits and updates ensure the system stays ahead of potential vulnerabilities.

- **Scalability and Performance:**

  - *Criticism*: Skeptics question whether the GlobeTrotter Ecosystem can efficiently handle the vast volume of transactions on a global scale without compromising speed or reliability.

  - *Response*: The Ecosystem's hybrid blockchain architecture is designed for high scalability, capable of processing millions of transactions simultaneously. This scalability is bolstered by the use of cutting-edge technology and infrastructure upgrades to accommodate growing demands.

- **User Privacy and Data Sovereignty:**

  - *Criticism*: The handling of personal data within a digital ecosystem raises concerns about user privacy and data exploitation.

  - *Response*: The GlobeTrotter Ecosystem prioritizes user privacy by implementing strict data protection policies, anonymizing personal data, and giving users control over their information. Blockchain's inherent transparency also plays a critical role in ensuring data integrity.

- **Regulatory Compliance and Legal Frameworks:**

  - *Criticism*: The innovative nature of the GlobeTrotter Ecosystem could clash with existing regulatory frameworks and legal jurisdictions.

  - *Response*: Engaging with regulatory bodies and policymakers is key. The Ecosystem is committed to working within legal frameworks, adapting to evolving regulations, and participating in dialogues to shape future policies.

- **Digital Divide and Accessibility:**

  - *Criticism*: The reliance on digital technology could exacerbate the digital divide, leaving behind those without access to necessary technology.

  - *Response*: The GlobeTrotter Ecosystem addresses this by providing free, secure smartphones and promoting digital literacy programs, ensuring that the benefits of the platform are accessible to all.

Future-Proofing the System

- **Continuous Innovation and Adaptation**: The Ecosystem is not static; it evolves continually, integrating new technologies and innovations to stay relevant and effective. This approach includes adopting emerging blockchain technologies, exploring quantum-resistant encryption methods, and staying abreast of technological advancements.

- **Building a Resilient Infrastructure**: Infrastructure resilience is paramount. This involves not only robust digital infrastructure but also redundancy systems and disaster recovery protocols to ensure uninterrupted service even in adverse conditions.

- **Global Collaboration and Partnerships**: Collaborating with tech companies and international organizations is crucial for harmonizing standards, sharing best practices, and promoting global acceptance.

- **User-Centric Design and Feedback Loop**: Keeping the user at the center of the Ecosystem's design ensures that it remains responsive to user needs and expectations. Regular feedback mechanisms, user forums, and community engagement ensure that the system adapts to changing user requirements.

- **Sustainability and Environmental Stewardship**: Commitment to sustainability is a core tenet. The Ecosystem actively seeks to minimize its environmental footprint and invest in sustainable technologies and practices.

- **Education and Awareness Campaigns**: Educating users and the public about digital currency, blockchain technology, and financial management is vital. This empowerment ensures informed participation and fosters a culture of financial literacy.

- **Scenario Planning and Risk Management**: Engaging in comprehensive scenario planning and proactive risk management enables the Ecosystem to anticipate and prepare for future challenges, whether they be technological, economic, or social.

In conclusion, while the GlobeTrotter Ecosystem faces its share of challenges and criticisms, its proactive and forward-thinking approach, combined with a commitment to continuous innovation and adaptation, positions it well to navigate these hurdles. By embedding resilience, inclusivity, and sustainability at its core, the Ecosystem is not just a financial platform but a beacon for the future of global currency.

Conclusion: Envisioning a New Era of Global Harmony

In the grand tapestry of the world's economic systems, the emergence of the GlobeTrotter Ecosystem stands as a monumental shift, one that promises to rewrite the rules of global finance and usher in an era of unprecedented harmony and interconnectedness. This standalone system, with its innovative approach, has the potential to reshape not just currency, but the very fabric of global society.

The Global Impact of the GlobeTrotter Ecosystem

- **Elimination of Traditional Banks and Central Banks:**

  - By replacing traditional banking infrastructure, the GlobeTrotter Ecosystem eradicates the historical complexities and inequalities perpetuated by these institutions. The world witnesses the dismantling of age-old financial barriers, leading to a more democratized and accessible economic landscape.

  - Without central banks, the concept of national currencies becomes obsolete, replaced by a singular, global currency that operates beyond the confines of national borders. This unified approach simplifies international trade and finance, making them more equitable and efficient.

- **Redistribution of Economic Power:**

  - The GlobeTrotter Ecosystem levels the economic playing field. Wealth is no longer concentrated in the hands of a few; rather, it is dispersed across the global population, fostering economic parity and reducing income inequality.

  - This redistribution sparks a surge in entrepreneurship and innovation, as individuals worldwide now have the resources and financial freedom to pursue their ambitions.

- **A Paradigm Shift in Economic Policy Making**: The decentralized nature of the GlobeTrotter Ecosystem ensures that economic policies are no longer dictated by a handful of policymakers. Instead, they are shaped by the collective will of the global populace, leading to policies that are more representative and fair.

- **Promotion of Global Stability and Peace**: As economic disparities diminish, so do the tensions and conflicts often fueled by these inequalities. The GlobeTrotter Ecosystem acts as a catalyst for peace, fostering a sense of global unity and cooperation.

Achieving Global Harmony Through Innovative Economic Systems

The GlobeTrotter Ecosystem is not just a financial model; it's a blueprint for a more harmonious world. It demonstrates that when economic systems are designed with equity, transparency, and inclusivity at their core, they can become powerful tools for social change.

- **Universal Access and Inclusivity**: This new era is marked by the universal accessibility of financial resources. No longer bound by geographical or socio-economic constraints, individuals from all walks of life can participate in the global economy on equal footing.

- **Environmental Consciousness and Sustainability**: The Ecosystem's minimal environmental footprint sets a new standard for sustainable economic practices, showing that financial prosperity does not have to come at the expense of our planet.

- **Empowering Communities**: With the redistribution of economic power, communities around the world are empowered to take charge of their development, leading to grassroots innovations and solutions tailored to local needs.

- **Reshaping Global Values**: The GlobeTrotter Ecosystem fosters a global culture that values cooperation over competition, collective well-being over individual wealth, and long-term prosperity over short-term gains.

- **A Beacon for Future Generations**: This new economic paradigm serves as a legacy for future generations—a world where financial systems are not instruments of control, but enablers of potential, creativity, and global unity.

As we stand at the threshold of this new era, the GlobeTrotter Ecosystem is more than just a revolutionary economic model; it's a beacon of hope. It represents the possibility of a world where economic systems are not just efficient and innovative but also fair and humane.

This vision of global harmony, achieved through groundbreaking economic mechanisms, is not just a distant dream but a tangible reality. As we embrace this new era, we embark on a journey of collective growth, prosperity, and peace—a journey towards a world where every individual has the opportunity to thrive, and the global community flourishes in unison.

In the pages of history, the GlobeTrotter Ecosystem will be remembered not just as a financial revolution, but as a testament to the enduring human spirit, our capacity for innovation, and our relentless pursuit of a better, more harmonious world.

Conclusion

Synthesizing Core Insights

As we journey through the enthralling world of digital currencies in this chapter, we uncover a trove of insights that promise to redefine our financial landscape. The exploration reveals a stark contrast between decentralized currencies and Central Bank Digital Currencies (CBDCs), each harboring its unique implications for the future of money.

Decentralized Currencies – The Emblem of Financial Liberation:

- Decentralized currencies, epitomized by the GlobeTrotter Ecosystem, are the vanguard of financial autonomy. They represent a seismic shift from traditional financial control, placing power squarely in the hands of the people. Their hallmark is the elimination of intermediaries, offering peer-to-peer transactions that are transparent, secure, and unbound by geographical or political constraints.

- In this decentralized world, the chains of financial gatekeepers are broken. Currency is no longer a tool of control by centralized entities but a means of empowerment. This system fosters an environment where innovation thrives, and the barriers to financial entry are dismantled, paving the way for a more inclusive economy.

Central Bank Digital Currencies (CBDCs) – A Blend of Old and New:

- In contrast, CBDCs represent a digital evolution of traditional fiat currencies, controlled and issued by central banks. They are a bridge between the old and the new, merging the familiarity of government-backed money with the efficiency of digital technology.

- While CBDCs offer enhanced transactional efficiency and potentially greater financial inclusion, they also retain elements of central control. They could herald a new era of financial surveillance and government oversight, raising concerns about privacy and the autonomy of individual spending.

The Dichotomy – Understanding the Future Financial Landscape:

- Understanding the dichotomy between decentralized currencies and CBDCs is pivotal in navigating the future financial landscape. It's a narrative of two paths diverging in a digital wood – one leading to a world where financial freedom and innovation are paramount, and the other to a more regulated, albeit modernized, financial ecosystem.

- This understanding is not just academic; it has profound implications for how we interact with money, how businesses operate, and how governments wield financial influence.

As we synthesize these core insights, we stand at a crossroads in financial history. The choice between decentralized currencies and CBDCs is more than just a preference for digital formats – it's about choosing between two fundamentally different visions of the future of money. One path leads to a world where financial freedom reigns supreme, and the other to a digitized extension of the current financial order. The decisions we make today will shape the financial world of tomorrow, and understanding these differences is key to navigating this brave new digital frontier.

Reflecting on the Evolution of Money

The evolution of money, a journey spanning centuries from tangible assets to digital currencies, stands as a testament to humanity's relentless pursuit of progress and efficiency. This transition, far from being merely a technological leap, symbolizes a profound transformation in the global financial paradigm, one that affects every aspect of our economic lives.

From Barter to Digital – A Tale of Progress:

- Imagine a world where transactions began with barter, a simple exchange of goods, evolving through the ages into coins and paper money, each step simplifying trade and broadening economic horizons. Now, we stand at the brink of the digital era, where money transcends physical boundaries, existing as bytes and data.

- The shift from tangible cash to digital currencies isn't just about convenience; it's a redefinition of what money is and can be. It's a transition from a static, physical entity to a dynamic, fluid form that can traverse the globe in seconds.

Impacts on Individual Autonomy:

- This evolution dramatically impacts individual autonomy in financial matters. Digital currencies, especially decentralized ones like those in the GlobeTrotter Ecosystem, provide unprecedented control over our own personal finances. They empower users with direct management of their assets, free from the oversight of central banks or the whims of government policies.

- Imagine being able to send money across the world without waiting for bank approvals or paying any fees. This newfound autonomy also brings responsibility – the responsibility of managing and securing one's digital wealth, a paradigm shift from relying on institutions for financial safety.

Redefining Global Economic Structures:

- On a macro scale, the emergence of digital currencies is redefining global economic structures. Decentralized currencies are challenging the traditional state-centric model, proposing a world where financial power is distributed among its users rather than concentrated in the hands of a few.

- This shift could lead to more equitable economic systems, where developing countries have direct access to global markets without the need for intermediary financial institutions, potentially reducing the economic disparity on a global scale.

The Broader Societal Implications:

- The societal implications of this evolution are profound. Digital currencies can potentially democratize finance, making it accessible to the unbanked populations of the world. They can drive innovation in sectors like e-commerce, remittances, and even governance, by introducing transparency and efficiency through blockchain technology.

- Moreover, this shift raises important questions about privacy, security, and regulation. As our financial lives become increasingly digital, protecting against cyber threats and ensuring ethical use of financial data become paramount concerns.

In reflecting on the evolution of money, it's clear that we are not just witnessing a change in the form of currency but a revolution in the very concept of financial exchange. This evolution represents a pivotal shift in the power dynamics of the global economy, opening up opportunities for greater autonomy, efficiency, and inclusivity. As we navigate this new digital financial landscape, we must tread with a balance of optimism and caution, embracing the possibilities while being acutely aware of the challenges and responsibilities that come with this new era of global currency.

The Future of Financial Technology and Society

The future of financial technology, particularly with the advent of blockchain and artificial intelligence (AI), is poised to reshape not only our banking systems but the very fabric of societal interactions with money. This profound transformation invites us to envisage a world where financial transactions are not just transactions but integrated experiences, deeply intertwined with every aspect of our daily lives.

Blockchain: The Bedrock of Tomorrow's Finance

- Picture a world where blockchain technology underpins every financial transaction. This isn't just about cryptocurrency; it's about the creation of a decentralized ledger that records everything from the purchase of your morning coffee to complex international trade agreements.

- The transparency and immutability of blockchain bring a new level of trust to transactions. Imagine buying a house with the entire history of the property, from construction to every transaction, accessible in an unalterable ledger. Such transparency could significantly reduce fraud and increase efficiency in property markets.

- Blockchain also democratizes finance. It enables peer-to-peer lending and microfinance opportunities, opening financial markets to those previously excluded. This could lead to a more equitable distribution of wealth and resources, especially in underdeveloped regions.

AI: The Personal Financial Assistant

- AI in finance is set to transform our relationship with money. Imagine an AI that not only helps you budget and invest but also predicts future financial trends, offering personalized advice based on your spending habits, goals, and the broader economic environment.

- AI could revolutionize risk assessment in lending, using vast amounts of data to make more accurate predictions about an individual's ability to repay loans, leading to more nuanced and fair credit scoring systems.

- In investment, AI's predictive analytics could provide insights into market trends, helping individuals and institutions make informed decisions. This could democratize investment, allowing ordinary people access to strategies and insights once reserved for elite investors.

Transformed Financial Institutions

- The role of traditional financial institutions is likely to evolve. Banks may become more like tech companies, focusing on creating financial platforms and ecosystems rather than just providing loans and holding deposits.

- The GlobeTrotter Ecosystem exemplifies this shift. It's not just a currency but a complete financial environment, where every participant is both a consumer and a contributor.

- We might see the rise of decentralized autonomous organizations (DAOs), where financial decisions are made by consensus among stakeholders, not a central board of directors. This could lead to more democratic and transparent financial institutions.

Societal Impacts

- The way individuals interact with money will undergo a profound change. With instant, secure, and low-cost transactions, the concept of "waiting for funds to clear" could become obsolete. This immediacy will influence everything from personal cash flow to global trade.

- Financial literacy will need to evolve. Understanding digital currencies, blockchain, and AI will become as fundamental as understanding checking accounts and credit scores are today.

- The potential societal impacts extend beyond finance. Blockchain technology could be used for secure voting systems, transparent supply chains, and even in healthcare for secure and efficient patient data management.

The Challenges Ahead

- However, this future is not without challenges. There are concerns about privacy, as AI and blockchain technologies require access to vast amounts of data. The risk of cyber attacks and the ethical use of AI in decision-making are also significant considerations.

- The regulatory landscape will need to adapt to these new technologies. Ensuring that this financial evolution benefits society as a whole, without widening existing inequalities, will be a key challenge for policymakers.

As we contemplate this future, it's clear that the convergence of blockchain, AI, and financial services is set to redefine not just how we transact, but also how we view the concept of value, wealth, and trust in a digital age. This future holds the promise of a more inclusive, efficient, and transparent global financial system, but it also calls for responsible innovation, thoughtful regulation, and a commitment to ensuring these technologies serve the greater good of society. The GlobeTrotter Ecosystem, as a standalone system in this future, symbolizes a leap into this new era - an era where financial technology is seamlessly integrated into the fabric of society, offering new opportunities for growth, equality, and global harmony.

Ethical and Social Implications of Digital Currencies

In the realm of digital currencies, the ethical and social implications are as profound as the technological innovations themselves. As we move away from traditional monetary systems towards decentralized digital currencies and Central Bank Digital Currencies (CBDCs), the landscape of financial ethics and societal norms is being redrawn, calling for a nuanced and comprehensive understanding of these changes.

Privacy in the Digital Age

- A paramount concern with digital currencies is the issue of privacy. Decentralized digital currencies like those proposed in the GlobeTrotter Ecosystem offer a level of anonymity akin to physical cash transactions. However, this privacy must be balanced against the need for transparency to prevent illegal activities.

- CBDCs, controlled by state entities, bring concerns over surveillance and the potential for governments to monitor and even control spending behavior. Ensuring that these digital currencies do not infringe upon individual privacy rights is crucial in their design and implementation.

Security: The Double-Edged Sword

- Security is a cornerstone of digital currencies, but it also presents significant challenges. Blockchain technology offers unprecedented security advantages, but it's not infallible. The rise of sophisticated cyberattacks necessitates constant vigilance and evolution of security protocols.

- CBDCs present a different set of security concerns, primarily related to the centralization of financial data. A breach in a CBDC system could have far-reaching consequences, affecting an entire nation's financial stability.

Equitable Access: Bridging the Digital Divide

- Digital currencies herald a new era of financial inclusion, offering access to financial services for those traditionally excluded from the banking system. However, this potential can only be realized if these technologies are made accessible to all strata of society.

- The risk of a digital divide is real. Not everyone has access to the internet or the latest technology. Ensuring equitable access to digital currencies is paramount, particularly for decentralized systems like the GlobeTrotter Ecosystem which aim to democratize finance.

Balancing Innovation with Regulation

- The regulatory landscape for digital currencies is still evolving. Regulators face the challenge of fostering innovation while protecting consumers and maintaining financial stability.

- Decentralized currencies operate on the fringes of this regulatory framework, offering freedom and innovation but also raising questions about legal recourse and consumer protection.

- CBDCs, on the other hand, are subject to strict regulation, but this control must be exercised responsibly to ensure that it doesn't stifle innovation or infringe upon individual freedoms.

The Social Contract of Money

- Money is more than a medium of exchange; it's a social contract. The shift to digital currencies changes this contract, affecting everything from individual autonomy to the role of the state in personal finances.

- The ethical and social implications of digital currencies extend to notions of trust, the value of money, and the role it plays in society. As we transition to these new forms of currency, it's vital to foster a dialogue around these topics, ensuring that the future of money aligns with the values and needs of society as a whole.

The Need for a Balanced Approach

- A balanced approach to the development of digital currencies is critical. This approach must weigh the benefits of innovation against the risks, ensuring that privacy, security, and equitable access are not sacrificed in the pursuit of technological advancement.

- As we navigate this new terrain, collaboration between technologists, regulators, ethicists, and the broader community is essential. Together, we can shape a financial future that is secure, private, inclusive, and aligned with the ethical standards that underpin a just and equitable society.

In conclusion, the ethical and social implications of digital currencies are as diverse and complex as the technologies themselves. As we embrace these new forms of money, we must do so with a conscious commitment to the values that define us as a society. By fostering open dialogue, collaborative innovation, and responsible regulation, we can ensure that the future of money reflects our collective aspirations for a fair, secure, and inclusive world.

Encouraging Ongoing Research and Collaboration

In this transformative era where digital currencies are reshaping the financial landscape, the call for ongoing research and collaboration resonates more profoundly than ever. The emergence and evolution of digital currencies, particularly in the context of the proposed GlobeTrotter Ecosystem, are not merely technological marvels but also intricate tapestries woven from various disciplines and perspectives. The need for interdisciplinary collaboration and relentless research is paramount to ensure that these innovations not only thrive but also integrate seamlessly into our global society.

Interdisciplinary Collaboration: A Symbiotic Necessity

- The world of digital currencies is where technology meets economics, policy intersects with societal norms, and futuristic ideas converge with practical realities. This intersectionality necessitates a collaborative approach involving experts from diverse fields.

- Technologists and software engineers are at the forefront, continuously innovating and refining blockchain and AI systems.

Yet, their efforts must be complemented by economists' insights into market dynamics and the socio-economic impact of digital currencies.

- Policymakers and legal experts play a crucial role in framing regulations that balance innovation with consumer protection and financial stability. Their involvement ensures that digital currencies operate within a framework that is both progressive and secure.

Continued Research: The Lifeline of Innovation

- The digital currency landscape is ever-evolving, with new challenges and opportunities emerging regularly. Continuous research is vital to stay ahead of these developments, be it in enhancing security protocols, improving user interfaces, or understanding the environmental impact of these technologies.

- Academic institutions, think tanks, and research organizations should be encouraged to delve deeper into digital currencies. Their independent and comprehensive studies can provide valuable insights, guiding the development and adoption of these technologies.

The Role of the GlobeTrotter Ecosystem in Fostering Collaboration

- As a standalone system, the GlobeTrotter Ecosystem is a microcosm of what global digital currency systems can achieve. It presents a unique opportunity for collaborative research and innovation, serving as a testbed for new ideas and technologies.

- The Ecosystem can facilitate partnerships between academia, industry, governments, and community organizations. Such partnerships can explore various facets of digital currencies, from technical aspects like blockchain scalability to more nuanced areas like the societal impact of a universal basic income facilitated through digital currency.

Engaging the Broader Community

- In the development of digital currencies, especially systems as holistic as the GlobeTrotter Ecosystem, the involvement of the end-users – the global community – is crucial. Public forums, surveys, and beta testing with diverse user groups can provide invaluable feedback, shaping the system to be more user-friendly and inclusive.

- Educational initiatives to increase digital literacy and understanding of digital currencies among the general population are also vital. This not only prepares individuals for the impending shift in the financial landscape but also empowers them to contribute to the discourse around these technologies.

Looking Towards the Future

- As we envisage the full realization and online integration of the GlobeTrotter Ecosystem, the journey is as significant as the destination. This journey, paved with research, collaboration, and interdisciplinary efforts, holds the key to unlocking the full potential of digital currencies.

- The future beckons with promises of a more inclusive, efficient, and transparent financial system. To reach this future, the concerted efforts of all stakeholders are necessary. We must foster an environment where continuous learning, open collaboration, and innovative thinking are not just encouraged but are the driving forces behind the evolution of digital currencies.

In conclusion, the advancement of digital currencies and the fruition of systems like the GlobeTrotter Ecosystem demand more than just technological prowess. They require a harmonious blend of knowledge, expertise, and perspective from various domains. It is through this collaborative and continuous pursuit of knowledge that we can steer the future of money towards a horizon that promises global harmony, financial inclusion, and an equitable digital economy for all.

Final Thoughts on Embracing Change and Uncertainty

As we stand at the precipice of a monumental shift in the financial world, our journey through the exploration of digital currencies brings us to a crucial realization: embracing change and navigating uncertainty are not just choices but necessities in today's dynamic financial landscape. The evolution from physical currencies to digital ones, spearheaded by innovations like the GlobeTrotter Ecosystem, represents a paradigm shift, a leap into a future where finance and technology merge in unprecedented ways.

The Inevitability of Change in Finance

- The history of money, from barter systems to gold coins, and now to digital currencies, is a testament to the constant evolution of financial systems. Each era of financial innovation has been met with skepticism and reluctance, yet change has proven not only inevitable but beneficial.

- Today, as digital currencies gain prominence, they challenge traditional notions of money, decentralizing control and democratizing financial participation. This shift requires us to be adaptable, to learn and unlearn, as we navigate through these transformative times.

Navigating Uncertainty with Open-mindedness

- The realm of digital finance, especially concepts like the GlobeTrotter Ecosystem, is rife with uncertainties and questions. How will these systems integrate with existing financial structures? What implications will they have on global economies? The answers to these questions are unfolding in real-time, requiring us to remain open-minded and flexible in our approach.

- Staying informed and educated about these emerging technologies is crucial. It involves engaging with new ideas, participating in discussions, and even experimenting with digital currencies. This proactive approach not only demystifies digital finance but also empowers us to be active participants in shaping its future.

Shaping the Future of Money

- The future of money, as envisioned in systems like the GlobeTrotter Ecosystem, is not a distant, abstract concept. It is a reality being molded by today's innovations and decisions. We, as individuals, have a role in shaping this future.

- By contributing to discussions about digital currencies, advocating for ethical practices, and supporting technologies that align with our values, we influence the trajectory of digital finance. It is through our collective efforts that a fair, inclusive, and transparent financial system can emerge.

Guarding Financial Freedom: The Imperative of Resisting Central Bank Digital Currencies

- As we navigate the vast and intricate landscape of digital finance, it becomes increasingly clear that the choices we make today will sculpt our financial future. One such critical decision lies in our stance towards Central Bank Digital Currencies (CBDCs). While they may appear as a step towards modernization, it is essential to approach them with caution and discernment. The prospect of CBDCs brings with it a potential for unprecedented surveillance and control over financial transactions, which could lead to a significant erosion of personal freedoms and privacy. This concern is not just theoretical; it is a tangible risk that could reshape the very fabric of our financial autonomy. Therefore, it is crucial for individuals and communities to stay informed, critically evaluate the implications of CBDCs, and advocate for financial systems that preserve individual rights and freedoms. By collectively voicing our concerns and actively participating in shaping the future of money, we can steer away from paths that might lead to restrictive financial environments and instead, champion for systems that uphold transparency, empowerment, and liberty for all. Remember, the power to mold the future of our financial system lies in our hands, and it is our responsibility to ensure that it evolves in a direction that enhances, rather than restricts, our freedom and autonomy.

Hope in a World Powered by the GlobeTrotter Ecosystem

- Envisioning a world where a system like the GlobeTrotter Ecosystem is a reality fills us with hope. It's a world where financial barriers are lowered, where every individual has access to global markets, and where financial transactions are secure, swift, and transparent.

- This hopeful future is not just a dream. It is a potential reality that can be achieved through innovation, collaboration, and a shared commitment to a better financial future for all.

Encouraging a Proactive Stance

- As we conclude our exploration, we encourage you, the reader, to be proactive in your journey through the world of digital finance. Stay curious, stay informed, and most importantly, stay engaged. The future of money is not just something that will happen to us — it is something we have the power to influence and shape.

A Beacon of Optimism

- In a world often clouded by economic disparities and financial crises, the GlobeTrotter Ecosystem stands as a beacon of optimism. It represents a collective aspiration for a financial system that serves everyone, not just the few. It embodies the spirit of innovation and the relentless pursuit of a more equitable world.

As we close this chapter, let's carry forward the spirit of exploration and the willingness to embrace change. The future of money, with all its complexities and uncertainties, is a canvas awaiting our collective creativity. It's time to be part of that change, to be part of a financial revolution that promises a brighter, more inclusive future for all. Let's step into this new era with hope, determination, and the belief that a system like the GlobeTrotter Ecosystem could one day illuminate the path towards global harmony.